SINGAPORE HERITAGE COOKBOOKS

MALAY HERITAGE
Cooking

SINGAPORE HERITAGE COOKBOOKS

MALAY HERITAGE
Cooking

RITA ZAHARA
Foreword by MDM ZURAIDAH ABDULLAH

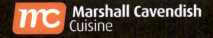

Editor: Lydia Leong
Designer: Bernard Go
Photographer: Hongde Photography

Copyright © 2012 Marshall Cavendish International (Asia) Private Limited
Reprinted 2013

This book is proudly sponsored by ATeR | ReTA and VisionInc.

The Publisher wishes to thank Noritake and Vantage for sponsoring the tableware used in this book.

This book is supported under the National Heritage Board's
Heritage Industry Incentive Programme (Hi²P)

Published by Marshall Cavendish Cuisine
An imprint of Marshall Cavendish International

All rights reserved

No part of this publication may be reproduced, stored in a retrieval system or transmitted, in any form or by any means, electronic, mechanical, photocopying, recording or otherwise, without the prior permission of the copyright owner. Request for permission should be addressed to the Publisher, Marshall Cavendish International (Asia) Private Limited, 1 New Industrial Road, Singapore 536196
Tel: (65) 6213 9300   Fax: (65) 6285 4871   E-mail: genref@sg.marshallcavendish.com
Online bookstore: http://www.marshallcavendish.com

Limits of Liability/Disclaimer of Warranty: The Author and Publisher of this book have used their best efforts in preparing this book. The Publisher makes no representation or warranties with respect to the contents of this book and is not responsible for the outcome of any recipe in this book. While the Publisher has reviewed each recipe carefully, the reader may not always achieve the results desired due to variations in ingredients, cooking temperatures and individual cooking abilities. The Publisher shall in no event be liable for any loss of profit or any other commercial damage, including but not limited to special, incidental, consequential, or other damages.

Other Marshall Cavendish Offices:

Marshall Cavendish Corporation. 99 White Plains Road, Tarrytown NY 10591-9001, USA • Marshall Cavendish International (Thailand) Co Ltd. 253 Asoke, 12th Flr, Sukhumvit 21 Road, Klongtoey Nua, Wattana, Bangkok 10110, Thailand • Marshall Cavendish (Malaysia) Sdn Bhd, Times Subang, Lot 46, Subang Hi-Tech Industrial Park, Batu Tiga, 40000 Shah Alam, Selangor Darul Ehsan, Malaysia.

Marshall Cavendish is a trademark of Times Publishing Limited

National Library Board, Singapore Cataloguing-in-Publication Data

Rita Zahara.
Malay heritage cooking / Rita Zahara ; foreword by Zuraidah Abdullah. – Singapore :
Marshall Cavendish Cuisine, c2012.
p. cm. – (Singapore heritage cookbooks)
Includes bibliographical references and index.
ISBN : 978-981-4328-66-1

1. Cooking, Singaporean. 2. Cooking, Malay. I. Title. II. Series: Singapore heritage cookbooks.

TX724.5.S55
641.595957 — dc22   OCN756147478

Printed in Singapore by KWF Printing Pte Ltd

DEDICATION

Lovingly dedicated in memory of my grandparents, Alal Mohamed Russull and Che Zahara Noor Mohamed.

> *Grandma, I am honoured to be named after you. Even though I did not get a chance to meet you, stories of you and grandpa linger and influence what I do today. It is important to me that you know how grateful I am for the legacy you left behind—your commitment to the country and community, your tremendous courage, strength, quiet resilience, wisdom, compassion and dedication. These things I will always carry with me wherever I go.*

I would also like to pay tribute to my beloved late mother, Hajjah Zabidah, my mentor, best friend, confidante and inspiration.

> *Mummy, I miss you. You left us in 2008, but not a day has gone by when I do not think about you. Your humility and world views have guided me. Your kindness still warms my heart and those of all who knew you. You shared dreams, inspired love, healed hearts and nurtured minds. You often reminded me to "remain useful, thoughtful and compassionate." I feel this with the utmost passion in my heart. I thank God every day for having blessed me with you as my mother. I can only aspire to be the role model that you were.*

This book is also dedicated to my father, Haji Mohamed Nazeer Alal Mohamed Russull. At 71 years old, he is still going strong and I am thankful that he is here to witness and be part of this project. He has committed his life to nurturing my sisters and me and for that I am eternally grateful.

> *My darling Ayah, thank you for being there for our family through every mountain high and every valley low. Thank you for always pushing us to do our best in everything we undertake. Without your invaluable encouragement, support and guidance, we would not be who we are today. Ayah, you have planted the trees so that we can enjoy shade over our heads. Your strong leadership, which we are fortunate to inherit, gives us a deep sense of comfort. We hope that you are happy to share the shade you have painstakingly created.*

To the world's greatest grandparents and parents, I love you. This book is for you.

Rita Zahara

CONTENTS

8   Foreword
10 Preface
20 Acknowledgements
22 Introduction

28 Basic Recipes
32 Appetisers & Light Meals
48 Rice & Noodles
80 Fish & Seafood
98 Meat & Poultry
120 Vegetables & Pickles
136 Cookies & Cakes
158 Snacks & Drinks

179 Glossary of Ingredients
185 Menu Suggestions
186 Weights & Measures
187 Resources
188 Index
190 Photo Credits
191 About the Author
192 Contributors

FOREWORD

Food often inspires our creativity and imagination. It is one of the key factors that identifies communities and brings people together from diverse backgrounds and cultures. It also creates a common experience such that wherever we are in the world, a familiar smell or name of a dish quickly reminds us of home and those dearest to us, our family.

In addition, the preparation and cooking of food is an integral process for the transmission of family values and culture over time. Family recipes are passed on, preserved and modified across generations. What's more, cooking together and sharing a meal have always been key activities that bonded families through thick and thin. This book gives testimony to that. The additional research and information provided within these pages also add value to our efforts in documenting the various aspects of the Malay community and its heritage in Singapore.

Most importantly, this book provides a unique insight into the life of one of our pioneers, Che Zahara Noor Mohamed, who founded the first Muslim women's welfare home in Singapore in 1947, known as the Malay Women's Welfare Association (MWWA).

May this book be a legacy that will continue to connect us to our heritage, making it relevant and an inspiration not just for the present generation, but for future generations to come.

Mdm Zuraidah Abdullah
Chairman
Malay Heritage Foundation

PREFACE

This book is an anthology of my family's roots and a celebration of Malay cuisine, recipes spanning three generations, passed down from my late grandmother to my late mother, and then to my sisters and me. For my family, food has always played a big role in preserving our culture and traditions, bonding people and serving others.

My grandmother is the daughter of Noor Mohamed who over a century ago, together with Sultan Ali of Singapore and Sultan Abubakar of Johor, were the first few Malays to study the English language at Cusbury's school, then situated at Zion Road. Upon graduation, my great-grandfather joined the government service. He was also an advisor to Sultan Ali. As one of the leading, prominent Malay figures in Singapore, he was asked to give a speech in English on behalf of the Malays, on the occasion of the Diamond Jubilee of Queen Victoria. He was also credited as the one who introduced the wearing of western trousers among Malay men, gaining the nickname, Encik Noor Mohamed Pantalón (*pantalón* is trousers in Spanish).

My great-grandfather's long advocacy for social welfare greatly influenced my grandmother and she devoted most of her time to looking after the welfare of the poor, the plight of the destitute, orphans and womenfolk. In 1947, she established the first Muslim women's welfare home in Singapore, known as the Malay Women's Welfare Association (MWWA). She was then elected as Founder President. In some circles, she became known as Che Zahara Kaum Ibu (Che Zahara who protected women and children). She also played a significant role in lobbying for the Women's Charter in Singapore. Her contributions to post-war Singapore and the Malay community will be documented and featured at the museum at the Malay Heritage Centre in 2012.

My grandfather, Alal Mohamed Russull (seated). One of his contributions to the community included entertainment. He owned Sri Rani Opera (Malay *bangsawan*). The picture displayed behind the telephone is of a play he financed called *Puteri Gunung Ledang* in the 1950s.

Che Zahara (last row, section on right, third from centre) represented Singapore at the International Women's and Children's Conference in Geneva, circa 1950.

Che Zahara (back row, middle) at the International Women's and Children's Conference in Geneva, circa 1950.

PREFACE | 11

Some of the protected women, orphans and social workers at the MWWA, 1948.

Open house at the MWWA's premises on the occasion of Prophet Muhammed's birthday, 1949.

The MWWA opened its doors every Friday to provide free food for all, circa 1950.

The MWWA's mission was to succour Malay women and children who, by force of circumstance, had been rendered helpless in the flow of social order. As a charitable organisation, the MWWA served with commendable zeal more than 300 women and orphans, providing them with money, shelter, jobs, training, religious education and much-needed moral support.

The role of Malay women was, by tradition, largely domestic. Che Zahara acknowledged that times were changing and stood up for women and children to have access to education. She believed that they could contribute positively to their families, communities and country. Che Zahara and her husband's acts of kindness and generosity in giving to the needy are partly recorded in this book. Che Zahara would cook and provide free food for the public every Friday. One of her signature dishes, *sambal jengganan Che Zahara Kaum Ibu* (page 122), is included in this book.

My late mother, having learnt to recite the Quran, taught it to children and adults, winding the stories and philosophies that she shared around her cooking. Most of her dishes are for everyday meals, with a handful suitable for serving to guests during small family parties, special occasions and large-scale community events. She participated actively in large-scale community events with

From left: My mother, Hajah Zabidah, adding the final touches for an event she was catering for, circa 1980; with my cousin (seated), aunties and mother preparing for a catering function. I was eight years old.

my father and used to donate food to charitable and fund-raising activities. She was also always willing to share her recipes with anyone who asked for them, without holding anything back.

With her innate generosity, kindness, humility, charm and hospitality, my mother always considered it an honour to be able to invite anyone to sample her cooking. Her penchant for food and her ability to cook garnered such a reputation that we had a constant stream of people who used to place orders for her food. Over 30,000 people have had the Hajjah Zabidah food experience—and this is no exaggeration. She cooked for Malay weddings, theme parties and other private functions. We had the pleasure of entertaining both local and foreign guests, dignitaries, television producers and celebrities. For some foreigners, her dishes served as an introduction to home-cooked Malay cuisine. Food orders came in daily and that became a training opportunity for my sisters and me. From as early as the age of 14, we were able to whip up a decent meal or dessert. Although my mother exacted extremely high standards, we are grateful for the way that she taught and guided us.

Cooking thus played a pivotal role in my family. It was through cooking that kitchen skills were passed down. Through my mother's food, we bonded. Inevitably, eating also became a communal activity in our home. The dining table was where everyone gathered to share a meal and their encounters during the day. My father always believed that those who turn the preparation of

Rita Zamzamah's wedding in 2007. My mother was not too well then, but she still managed to organise and plan for the wedding.

family recipes into lively affairs would find the experience most rewarding. It was also through food that my mother expressed her love for us. Whenever any of us did well in school, there would be an eclectic range of food on the table. "Chase those rainbows," she would encourage us, so that we would attempt the improbable. She showed strength until the end and always had some enlightening words for us. The dishes my mother cooked were more than just food—there was a sense of sincerity, something truly honest in the way she prepared her food. She cooked with love and from the heart.

Two years after my mother passed away, I reflected on the lessons she had imparted to me. She had left behind scores of recipes accompanied by beautiful memories. During a visit to Marshall Cavendish's office in Singapore, a close family friend, Steve Dawson, encouraged me to publish her recipes and kitchen secrets. I have always wanted to pay tribute to my late grandmother and mother so as to continue the spirit of sharing that they sparked in me. It is with this intention that I have written this book. Although I am the main author of this book, I am heartened to have my sisters' support and contribution in various ways, from researching the details of the ingredients to recording some of their personal experiences with the dishes. We have tried our best to capture the essence of our grandmother's and mother's cooking, recreating some familiar, traditional dishes with subtle updates in style.

Hari Raya 2011. Father and daughters. From left: Rita Zamzamah, Rita Zarina, Mohamed Nazeer, Rita Zahara and Rita Zuhaida.

About the Recipes

The heart of Malay cuisine is not uniform from one generation to the next and the cultural mosaic of Malays today also varies from one household to another. While there have been slight modifications, the essence of Malay cooking, however, ultimately does not change. Generally, most Malay food is unpretentious and simple and, at the same time, a joy to eat. However, for any short-term visitor to Singapore, it can be quite tricky to navigate a menu in order to fully capture the best of Malay cuisine. Every meal has a story. Hence, this book aims to take you through a wonderful culinary journey. The recipes in this book come with headnotes that briefly describe the essence of each dish and its place in Malay cuisine and culture. At the same time, it is also important to understand that given Singapore's immigrant society, some dishes have been adapted from other ethnicities. This is especially true in our family, as cultural exchanges between our mother (Malay and Bugis) and our father's (Ceylonese) descent have made our family kitchen a culinary melting pot. The fragrance of Malay herbs and the exuberance of Indian spices co-exist in our home, as they do in many contemporary Malay homes. Traditional Malay ingredients such as dried prawn (shrimp) paste (*belacan*) and tamarind are enhanced with the use of traditional Indian ingredients such as banana leaves, cardamom, curry leaves and curry powder.

Thus, our mother created her own unique cooking style, steeped in social and cross-cultural lore. She studied old recipes and tweaked them into more contemporary styles of Malay cooking, finding new ways to prepare traditional food. Her kitchen was a curious blend of old and new: the electric blender next to the granite mortar and pestle; the microwave oven next to a well-seasoned wok.

The cultural exchange in the kitchen has led to a number of unique dishes modified by my mother, such as *bol kentang Hajjah Zabidah* (page 100), *laksa Johor nani* (page 76), *roti mariam* (page 40), *samosa daging berempah* (page 44) and *santan durian* (page 162). This book also features renowned traditional favourites such as *sate ayam* (page 34), *nasi lemak* (page 50), *sambal tumis udang* (page 94), *sambal goreng* (page 112), *rendang daging* (page 104) and *lontong sayur lodeh* (page 58) and classic Malay desserts such as *kuih tart klasik* (page 140) and *kek kukus* (page 150). You will also find more contemporary dishes such as *nasi pulau* (page 62), *mee telur daging* (page 78), *ikan sumbat berlada* (page 84), *udang bakar* (page 92), *mahshi kobis* Hubaba (page 130) and *kek brownies tiga-coklat kacang walnut* (page 156). These dishes are just some of the exciting Malay recipes that now form an integral part of Singapore's fascinating food scene.

In featuring these dishes, we have used the original, ethnic names of the various foods. We have also made every effort to include some authentic plates, tableware, exquisite fabrics, traditional accessories and other implements that have been intertwined in Malay history for centuries. Additionally, as these recipes have been carefully selected for the use in home kitchens, some methods have been simplified. Substitutes and cooking tips are provided where applicable and a glossary of ingredients and suggestions for putting together a meal for various occasions complete the book.

Losing someone is never easy. I think of my mother every day, but it gets better with time as I remember her more lovingly. The aroma from her dishes evoke memories of my childhood. It makes me feel that she is always with me. I hope this book will inspire you with its pictures, quotations and personal accounts. I invite you to share the delights of this special collection of recipes with as much joy as I had in preparing them.

My father and all his grandchildren on his 70th Birthday celebration, 2010. Clockwise from left: Muhd Syafiq Asyraf, Syed Muhd Luqman, Muhd Syafiq Akmal, Muhd Syafiq Arsyad, Sharifah Nadhrah, Muhd Syafiq Arish, Mohamed Nazeer, Nadya Naori Ikeda.

Reflections from the Heart

I grew up watching my parents devote a major part of their lives to the country, the community and anyone who came to them for help. My late parents and my late wife touched so many lives and they did so with competence, compassion and without expectations. They are my unsung heroes. They remain the perfect role models to me, my children and grandchildren. This tribute is an honour to my family. My only wish is that my grandchildren see a glimpse of the love in the hearts of their ancestors and may that love shine bright and guide them. Nobody can take the place of these extraordinary people in our lives.

Mohamed Nazeer Bin Alal Mohamed Russull

My mother was the best multitasker I've ever known. She was a disciplinarian, a teacher, an event planner, a great cook, a friend and a confidante. She wore many hats to raise the four of us and her cooking was one of the ways in which she demonstrated her love for us. She was ever ready to help others and would always put others before herself. Her selfless nature made her someone who was simply unforgettable to anyone who knew her. She may no longer be with us, but her views, thoughts and wisdom will always be a guiding light for me and my family.

Rita Zarina

It is not only through her culinary skills that my mother impressed me. A lady of few words, she exemplified how the true strength of a woman is not only revealed through her words but mostly through her actions. My mother dedicated her life to serving others, be it her family, friends or students, and had little time for herself. She lived to better the lives of others and that is the value she had carved in my soul. Even after leaving us, my mother will always be a source of inspiration, a devoted and capable wife and mother, selfless, loving and generous.

Rita Zamzamah

My mother was not a congresswoman, a philanthropist or an entrepreneur geared to move the economy. But in her modest little ways and in her unassuming manner, she made an impact on small groups of people, with her heart full of grace and a soul filled with love. The values she imbued in us have been held sacrosanct. Her unwavering spirit of giving and sharing comport with her broader concerns for humanity. She would say, "If you cannot alleviate poverty, then give a dollar. If you cannot be an advocate for world peace, be good to your neighbours." Her zeal and zest have inspired me to work fervently towards realising my dreams. To our Queen of Hearts, we deeply miss you.

Rita Zuhaida

ACKNOWLEDGEMENTS

This book would not have been possible without the support of the team at Marshall Cavendish International (Asia), namely, General Manager and Publisher Chris Newson, for his vision, the one ingredient without which nothing will cohere in this book. My editor, Lydia Leong, for her patience, creativity and diligence to make things look as perfect as they could be. A special mention also goes to Bernard Go and Tammy Rip, as well as Hong De of Hong De Photography. Our partnership and endeavour to produce the definitive reference to Malay heritage cuisine will not have materialised without your commitment and dedication to your craft.

An honourable mention goes to Mdm Zuraidah Abdullah, Julina Khusaini and the curators at the Malay Heritage Foundation for their enthusiasm and support throughout the production process of this book.

Special thanks go to Mr Alex Toh and Mr Kevin Ng who sponsored the tableware from Noritake. My sincere appreciation also goes to Dato Steven and Mdm Mashitah Haji Husain for sponsoring the tableware from Vantage. I am also grateful to Madam Sultanah and her two assistants, Ida Shariff and Sharifah Shida from Sultanah Bridal and Boutique and my long-time friend, Jeremy, from Fox Salon for helping with the outfits and make-up for the portrait shots for my sisters and I.

I would also like to thank those who assisted with the props for the photography session: Shahizan Bin Shahlan for the loan of his exquisite keris and delicate fabrics; Jamaludin Malik Bin Attan for the loan of Sultan Abubakar of Johor's artefacts; Shariffah Suhailah Alhady for the loan of the authentic plates and traditional tableware and Mdm Som Said for providing the traditional props and implements.

I also wish to express my deepest gratitude to my family: my father, Mohamed Nazeer, my mother-in-law, Shariffah Suhailah Alhady, my husband, Mohd Syed Jamal Alhadi, my children, Syed Muhammad Luqman and Sharifah Nadhrah for their kind understanding and endless support. I would also not have been able to do this without the love and support of my sisters, Rita Zarina and her family, Rita Zamzamah and her family and Rita Zuhaida, and my relatives and close friends who helped in immeasurable ways. Special thanks also to my assistant in the kitchen, Sutriah.

I would also like to express my sincere appreciation to my three muses, RW, FG and FL for continuously urging me to write and publish my writings and for inspiring me to explore the workings of my mind, my best friend, Jerrica Chooi for believing in me and being there for me since our secondary school days, Steve Dawson for his invaluable guidance and advice, my mother's godsons, Daud Yusof and Adi Rahman, and Syed Zafilen and Mas who helped me in Kuala Lumpur.

Rita Zahara

INTRODUCTION

The Evolving Malay Community

When Sir Stamford Raffles founded modern Singapore in 1819, the fishing village was already inhabited by an indigenous Malay population. This population grew with arrivals from neighbouring countries including Indonesia (ethnic Sumatrans, Javanese and Baweanese) and what was then known as Malaya (ethnic Malays), as well as the Middle East (ethnic Arabs). This multi-heritage phenomenon was and continues to be intensified by the prevalence of inter-ethnic (amongst Malays, Arabs, Sumatrans, Javanese, Baweanese, etc.) and interracial marriages (with Singapore's other immigrant groups especially the Chinese and Indians). Globalisation, with increased human mobility and international migration, has also generated an increase in international marriages. Thus, the Malay community in Singapore, which makes up 13.4 per cent of the country's population today, according to a population census taken in 2010 by the Singapore Department of Statistics, is diverse, with a mix of backgrounds and places of origin. Yet, despite the diversity of the past, Singaporean Malays strongly identify themselves as a racial group, bonded by a common religion and language.

Malay houses on stilts, 1907.

The Malays in Singapore remain a close-knit community even as they simultaneously interact with and contribute to the vibrancy of Singapore's cosmopolitan society. The camaraderie within the community is most observable during social events and gatherings. For instance, during Hari Raya Puasa (Eid ul-Fitr), it is common to see Malay families visiting one another dressed in beautifully designed and sometimes colour-coordinated *baju kurung* (Malay traditional costume). A wide variety of food ranging from traditional dishes to cakes and cookies is prepared by the hosts for their guests. The Malay wedding is another testimony of the community's collective identity. Marriages are often celebrated in an elaborate fashion, involving a large number of guests. Preparations for a wedding are usually undertaken by family members and close friends within the community, in the spirit of *gotong royong* (cooperation).

While some may suggest that globalisation flattens cultures and homogenises indigenous identities into a global one, the Malay community in Singapore is a perfect example of how cultural evolution does not imply a disconnection from heritage. For this community, the past continues to anchor, influence and inspire the future.

Hari Raya Puasa 2002. Boys in colour-coordinated *baju kurung*. From left: Muhd Syafiq Asyraf, Muhd Syafiq Arsyad, Syed Muhd Luqman and Muhd Syafiq Akmal.

The cooks and staff at the MWWA cooked regularly for public events since its opening in 1947.

Malay Cuisine

Malay cuisine in Singapore is a reflection of the country's multifaceted heritage and culture. It is strongly influenced by Indonesian and Malaysian cuisines and has infused elements from the various ethnic communities in Singapore's immigrant society. This book incorporates recipes passed down from one generation to another and reproduces the traditional elements of the past while mirroring the tastes of the present.

Today, rice continues to be the staple in Malay cuisine. It is eaten for breakfast, lunch and dinner. It is usually served warm as plain steamed rice or as flavoured varieties such as *nasi jagung* (page 64) and *nasi pulau* (page 62). A typical meal will consist of a mound of freshly cooked rice and small amounts of two or three other dishes as an accompaniment to the rice. These dishes can be vaguely categorised by several common tastes including *masak cili* (chilli-based), *masak lemak* (coconut-based), *masak asam* (tamarind-based), *masak merah* (tomato-based) and *masak kunyit* (turmeric-based). At the same time, an interesting characteristic of Malay cuisine is that some dishes offer clever blends of seemingly contradictory tastes. This is observable in the spicy

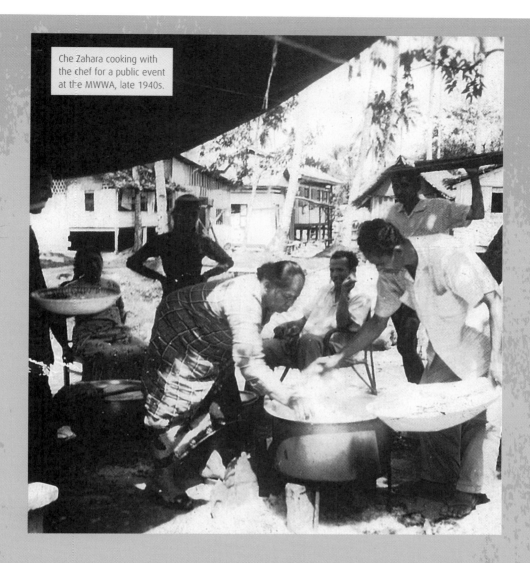

Che Zahara cooking with the chef for a public event at the MWWA, late 1940s.

yet sweet *ayam masak merah* (page 118), the spicy yet sour *asam pedas ikan* (page 82) and the spicy yet coconut-rich *ketam masak lemak cili padi* (page 90). Key ingredients for Malay dishes include fresh and dried chillies, coconut milk, tamarind, turmeric, onion, ginger, garlic, galangal and lemon grass. Although Malay cuisine is typically spicy, the rice and accompanying dishes are still often further accompanied by chilli-based condiments such as *sambal belacan* (page 31).

While the characteristics of Malay cuisine described above are still dominant today, it now also blends many elements of the various ethnic communities. Malay dishes such as *mee rebus* (page 72) and *soto ayam* (page 68) include Hokkien noodles, an ingredient adopted from the Chinese community, in the gravy/soup. *Tahu goreng* (page 42) consists of deep-fried bean curd, an ingredient mostly used in Chinese dishes, topped with bean sprouts and a spicy peanut sauce. Malay cuisine has also become a melting pot of herbs and spices—spices being most closely associated with Indian cuisine. It is no longer surprising to use curry leaves, once used only in Indian cooking, in Malay dishes. Ghee, a traditional Indian ingredient, is also used in some Malay pastries and cookies.

Apart from this fusion, Malay cuisine has also adapted dishes popularised by other ethnic communities, especially the Indians and Chinese. These include *kari ayam Melayu* (page 116), from Indian chicken curry and *nasi ayam* (page 54), from Chinese chicken rice. Amid such evolution, one characteristic remains constant—Malay cuisine in Singapore generally does not contain pork, in accordance with Muslim dietary restrictions. And even with the creation of a host of contemporary dishes, many classic Malay dishes remain today. Dishes such as *sate* (page 34) and *lontong sayur lodeh* (page 58) will not be easily nudged aside by some young and fashionable newbie at the dining table.

Food Etiquette

At the dining table, all dishes including the rice are served at the same time and not in the form of courses. Diners scoop the warm rice onto their plates and then help themselves to the dishes. Dessert is the only course that is served on its own towards the end of the meal. Before starting the meal, it is polite for diners to invite the more senior ones at the table to begin eating first by saying *jemput makan* (please eat). In an occasion when two diners reach out for the same dish, it is also polite to allow the more senior person to help himself first.

Traditionally, the Malays eat without cutlery, using the right hand. Only the fingers are used and the palm is kept clean. Diners wash their hands prior to eating as maintaining good hygiene is of utmost importance. In Malay social gatherings or restaurants, it is thus common to provide bowls of warm water or the *ketor* (a jug containing clean water accompanied by a big bowl) for rinsing the hands. While eating, one should only touch the food on one's plate and not the common dishes. It is considered impolite to overload one's plate with food at the first serving. It is also rude to leave food uneaten and even more so to return half-eaten food to the common serving dishes.

Even with modernisation, food etiquette for the Malays in Singapore continues to provide parameters for social behaviour. For this community especially, meal times are opportunities for socialising, be it as families or as larger social networks. Food etiquette at the dining table thus not only promotes the community's cultural heritage and values, but also strengthens the community's identity through the propagation of accepted behaviour.

My mother, Hajah Zabidah (bottom right) at a family gathering, circa 1970.

Guests were seated on the floor and dishes were served on big enamel trays at weddings, circa 1970.

BASIC RECIPES

Plain Rice 30

Sambal Kacang 30

Traditional Lontong 31

Sambal Belacan 31

PLAIN RICE

Long grain rice 320 g (11½ oz), rinsed
Water 320 ml (10⅔ fl oz)
Pandan leaf (optional) 1, tied into a knot

1. Place rice, water and pandan leaf in a rice cooker to cook. Rice is cooked when water is completely absorbed and rice is fluffy. Makes about 4 regular servings.

NOTE
- If not using a rice cooker, place rice, water and pandan leaf in a heavy saucepan. Bring to the boil, then lower heat and let rice simmer until water is completely absorbed and rice is fluffy.

SAMBAL KACANG

Vegetable oil as needed
Lemon grass 2 stalks, ends trimmed
Galangal 5-cm (2-in) knob, peeled
Palm sugar (*gula melaka*) 250 g (9 oz), finely chopped
Tamarind pulp 100 g (3½ oz), mixed with 250 ml (8 fl oz / 1 cup) water and strained
Coarsely ground peanuts 300 g (11 oz)
Salt to taste

Ground Paste
Dried chillies 10, soaked to soften, then cut into short lengths
Garlic 4 cloves, peeled
Onions 2, peeled and chopped

1. Prepare ground paste. Combine all ingredients in a blender and process into a paste.
2. Heat some oil in a heavy saucepan over medium heat. Add ground paste and stir-fry until lightly browned and fragrant.
3. Add whole lemon grass stalks and galangal knob and continue to stir-fry until mixture is lightly browned.
4. Add palm sugar and tamarind juice. Stir until well combined.
5. Stir in ground peanuts. Season with salt to taste. Stir and bring to the boil.
6. Remove from heat. Serve as an accompaniment to *sate ayam* (page 34) and *lontong sayur lodeh* (page 58).

TRADITIONAL LONTONG

Long grain rice as needed

Banana leaves as needed, cut into sheets about 25 x 15-cm (9 x 6-in)

Bamboo skewers as needed, cut into 5-cm (2-in) lengths

Water as needed

1. Place sufficient rice to fill about two-thirds of each banana leaf and roll up tightly. Fold in the edges of the banana leaves to prevent the rice from spilling out. Fasten with cut bamboo skewers.
2. Repeat to make as many parcels as desired.
3. Using a pot large enough to hold parcels, boil water and add rolls. Boil for 2½–3 hours until rice is thoroughly cooked.
4. Allow to cool before cutting and serving.

NOTE
- Ready-made or instant *lontong* is available at some supermarkets.

SAMBAL BELACAN

Dried prawn (shrimp) paste (*belacan*) 10 g (⅓ oz)

Red chillies 7

Red bird's eye chillies 3

Salt to taste

Sugar to taste

Limes 2, juice extracted, zest thinly sliced

1. Heat a small frying pan and dry-fry dried prawn paste for a few minutes until fragrant.
2. Using a mortar and pestle, pound dried prawn paste with chillies until well combined. Remove to a small bowl.
3. Season with salt and sugar to taste. Add freshly squeezed lime juice and lime zest.

NOTE
- *Sambal belacan* is typically served as an accompaniment to most Malay dishes.

APPETISERS & LIGHT MEALS

Sate Ayam 34
Ayam Goreng Berempah 36
Epok-Epok Daging 38
Roti Mariam 40
Tahu Goreng 42
Samosa Daging Berempah 44

SATE AYAM

Makes 30–40 sticks

This richly-flavoured meat, skewered on thin bamboo sticks and grilled, is best prepared to order and eaten on the spot. My parents used to sell *sate* during charity and fund-raising events, funfairs, birthday parties and special functions. On a typical day, they could sell between 1,000 and 3,000 sticks. A typical serving comprises 10 sticks with *ketupat* or *lontong*, slices of shallots, cucumber and *sambal kacang* (peanut gravy). My role during such events was to grill the *sate* with my dad. Charcoal does not burn well unless fanned vigorously. Hence, it is a two-handed job—*sate* sticks in the left hand and the fan in the right.

Skinless chicken thighs 500 g (1 lb 1 1/2 oz), cut into thin strips or cubes

Bamboo skewers as needed, soaked in water for 30 minutes before use

Castor sugar 1 Tbsp

Vegetable oil as needed

Lemon grass 1, bruised

Shallots 5–6, peeled and cut into wedges

Cucumber 1, cut into wedges

Lontong (page 31) 1, sliced or *ketupat*

Spice Paste

Coriander seeds 1 tsp, soaked for 10 minutes; drained before use

Fennel seeds 1/2 tsp, soaked for 10 minutes; drained before use

Ground cumin 1/2 tsp, soaked for 10 minutes; drained before use

Lemon grass 2 stalks, ends trimmed and minced

Galangal 2.5-cm (1-in) knob, peeled and sliced

Ginger 5-cm (2-in) knob, peeled and sliced

Onion 1, peeled and sliced

Garlic 3 cloves, peeled

Marinade

Ground turmeric 1 tsp

Sugar 1 Tbsp

Brown sugar 2 tsp

Tamarind pulp 2 tsp, mixed with 3 Tbsp water and strained

Vegetable oil 1 tsp

Raw skinned peanuts 50 g (1 2/3 oz), ground

Salt 1/2 tsp or to taste

1. Prepare spice paste. Combine all ingredients in a blender and process into a paste.
2. Prepare marinade. In a mixing bowl, combine spice paste with ground turmeric, sugars, tamarind juice, oil and ground peanuts. Rub marinade over chicken and season with salt. Leave to stand for at least 4 hours, if not overnight.
3. Thread marinated chicken through bamboo skewers, filling up to one-third of each skewer. Set skewers aside.
4. Dissolve castor sugar in a small bowl of oil. Grill *sate* over very hot charcoal or a grill and baste occasionally using bruised lemon grass dipped in the sugared oil. Keep turning *sate* to cook evenly.
5. Serve *sate* hot with *sambal kacang* (page 30), shallots, cucumber and *ketupat* or *lontong*.

NOTE

- Chicken can be substituted with other meat such as beef or mutton.
- Soaking the skewers before using reduces the chances of burning the sticks while grilling.

APPETISERS & LIGHT MEALS 35

AYAM GORENG BEREMPAH

Serves 4–6

One of the simplest yet tastiest Malay dishes is fried chicken and there are so many versions worth trying. What follows is my mother's special, yet simple recipe, much loved by my family. Delectably crisp and bursting with the robust flavours of half a dozen herbs and spices, this spicy fried chicken is scrumptious and the garnish of crumbs makes it extra special. Serve with plain rice for an even more divine experience.

Chicken 1, medium, cut into 8–12 pieces
Salt to taste
Vegetable oil as needed, for deep-frying

Marinade
Dried chillies 15, soaked to soften, then cut into short lengths
Coriander seeds 2 Tbsp
Cumin seeds 1 tsp, soaked for 10 minutes; drained before use
Fennel seeds 1 tsp, soaked for 10 minutes; drained before use
Garlic 7 cloves, peeled
Ground turmeric 1 Tbsp

1. Prepare marinade. Combine all ingredients for marinade, except ground turmeric, in a blender and process into a paste.
2. Transfer paste to a mixing bowl and mix in ground turmeric. Rub paste over chicken and season to taste with salt. Set aside for at least 1 hour.
3. Heat oil in a wok or deep frying pan over medium-high heat.
4. Deep-fry chicken in batches until golden brown and crisp. Drain well.
5. When done cooking, strain oil for crumbs and use to garnish chicken. Serve warm.

EPOK-EPOK DAGING

Makes 25–30 pieces

There are several types of Malay puffs and *epok-epok* is by far the most common. It can be stuffed with different fillings ranging from potatoes to sardines to meat. In some ways, my mother's *epok-epok* filling is similar to her samosa filling (page 44) but slight differences make each of them unique. While we were growing up, my mother used to get orders of at least 100 *epok-epok* a day. Her *epok-epok* was a popular staple on the menu, together with *nasi lemak* (page 50) and *onde-onde* (page 164). She would single-handedly prepare at least five different dishes daily. Whenever we had a chance to help her, each of us would be assigned different duties. One of my favourite roles was to crimp the edges of the puffs—an art form in itself.

Vegetable oil as needed

Filling
Potatoes 200 g (7 oz), peeled and diced
Ginger 5-cm (2-in) knob, peeled and thinly sliced
Minced beef 500 g (1 lb 1½ oz)
Beef curry powder 2 Tbsp
Onions 2, large, peeled and diced
Salt to taste
Sugar to taste

Coriander leaves (cilantro) 10 g (⅓ oz), finely chopped
Spring onions (scallions) 10 g (⅓ oz), finely chopped

Dough
Salt 1 tsp
Lukewarm water 250 ml (8 fl oz / 1 cup)
Margarine/ghee/butter 2 Tbsp
Vegetable oil 2 Tbsp
Plain (all-purpose) flour 500 g (1 lb 1½ oz)

1. Prepare filling. Boil diced potatoes for about 5 minutes. Drain and set aside. Using a mortar and pestle, pound ginger into a paste.
2. Heat 2 Tbsp oil in a wok over medium heat. Add ginger paste and stir-fry until fragrant. Add minced beef and stir-fry until meat changes colour. Add curry powder.
3. Add onions and stir-fry for about 5 minutes. Add potatoes gently until mixture is well combined before removing from heat. Stir in coriander leaves and spring onions. Season with salt and sugar to taste. Dish out and drain excess liquid from filling. Set aside to cool.
4. Prepare dough. In a large mixing bowl, stir salt into lukewarm water until dissolved. Add margarine/ghee/butter and oil. Sift flour into a large mixing bowl. Add water and oil mixture a little at a time until mixture comes together. Continue to knead until dough is smooth and does not stick to fingers.
5. Form dough into balls, each about 4-cm (1½-in) in diameter. Cover with plastic wrap or a clean kitchen towel and allow dough to rest for at least 30 minutes.
6. On a floured work surface, roll a dough ball into a thin circle using a rolling pin. Spoon some filling into the centre and fold pastry into a semi-circle to enclose filling. Crimp edges to seal. Repeat until ingredients are used up.
7. Heat some oil for deep-frying over low heat. Deep-fry *epok-epok* in batches until golden brown. Drain excess oil and serve hot.

NOTE
- Instead of crimping the *epok-epok* manually, you can use a curry puff mould.

ROTI MARIAM

Makes 6 pieces

Roti mariam is one of my mother's signature dishes. The crispy puff perfectly complements the soft filling of eggs and vegetables. This unique taste makes it a versatile dish suitable as an afternoon snack or a meal on its own. My eldest sister, Rita Zarina, whose husband is in the restaurant business, popularised my mother's *roti mariam* in Putrajaya, Malaysia. The dish caught the attention of many ministerial officials who worked in the area and garnered such a reputation that it was featured in a Malaysian newspaper.

Vegetable oil as needed

Filling

Dried prawns (shrimps) 80 g ($2^{4}/_{5}$ oz), soaked for 10 minutes; drained before use

Prawns (shrimps) 10, medium, peeled and deveined, cut into 1-cm ($^{1}/_{2}$-in) pieces

Onions 4, peeled and cut into cubes

Eggs 5, beaten

Green chillies 3, sliced

Coriander leaves (cilantro) 30 g (1 oz), sliced

Spring onions (scallions) 30 g (1 oz), sliced

Salt to taste

Dough

Lukewarm water 210 ml (7 fl oz)

Salt 1 tsp or to taste

Butter or ghee 2 Tbsp

Egg 1, beaten

Plain (all-purpose) flour 500 g (1 lb $1^{1}/_{2}$ oz)

1. Prepare filling. Drain dried prawns and use a mortar and pestle to crush them.
2. Heat some oil in a pan and stir-fry crushed dried prawns until lightly browned. Add fresh prawns and onions and cook until lightly browned and fragrant.
3. Add eggs and allow eggs to cook for a few minutes before stirring gently.
4. Add chillies, coriander leaves and spring onions. Continue to stir until well combined. Season to taste with salt. Dish out and drain excess liquid from filling. Set aside to cool.
5. Prepare dough. In a small bowl, mix lukewarm water with salt until completely dissolved.
6. In a mixing bowl, thoroughly mix salty water with butter or ghee and egg. Add flour gradually and knead until mixture comes together. Continue to knead until dough is smooth and does not stick to fingers.
7. Divide dough evenly into 6 balls. Cover with a plastic wrap. Leave to rest for about 30 minutes.
8. On a lightly floured work surface, roll a ball of dough out into a circle 8–10 cm (3–4-in) in diameter. Press out to an even thickness, then spread filling evenly on one side. Fold pastry into a semi-circle to enclose filling. Crimp edges to seal. Repeat until ingredients are used up.
9. Heat oil over medium-high heat. Deep-fry puffs in small batches until golden brown and crisp. Drain well.
10. Cut puffs into 2 or 3 parts and serve with chilli sauce.

TAHU GORENG

Serves 4

Tahu goreng is a dish of deep-fried firm bean curd with bean sprouts, sliced cucumber and sweet peanut sauce. It can be served as a side dish with other dishes or as a meal on its own. The key to a good *tahu goreng* is the firm bean curd. It has to be fresh. When the bean curd is deep-fried, it develops a crisp outer crust and remains creamy on the inside. My mother's peanut sauce has a nice balance of sweet, salty, spicy and sour flavours. This simple dish is also one my dad's favourite foods.

Vegetable oil as needed, for deep-frying
Firm bean curd 4 pieces
Bean sprouts 200 g (7 oz), blanched
Cucumber 1, finely sliced into strips

Ground Paste
Red bird's eye chillies 5
Dried prawn (shrimp) paste (*belacan*) 40 g (1$\frac{1}{3}$ oz)
Garlic 5 cloves, peeled

Peanut Sauce
Raw shelled peanuts 250 g (9 oz), roasted, skinned and finely ground
Water 200 ml (7 fl oz)
Tamarind pulp 50 g (1$\frac{2}{3}$ oz), mixed with 100 ml (3$\frac{1}{2}$ fl oz) water and strained
Sweet soy sauce 4 Tbsp
Black prawn (shrimp) paste 1$\frac{1}{2}$ Tbsp
Sugar 2 tsp
Salt $\frac{1}{8}$ tsp

1. Prepare ground paste. Using a mortar and pestle, pound bird's eye chillies into a paste. Using a blender, process dried prawn paste and garlic into a paste. Combine both pastes.
2. Prepare peanut sauce. Mix ground peanuts with water. Add tamarind juice, sweet soy sauce, black prawn paste, sugar and salt until well combined. Simmer gently in a small saucepan until a thick gravy forms. Takes about 5 minutes. Do not bring to the boil. Set aside.
3. Heat oil for deep-frying and deep-fry firm bean curd, turning once, until golden on all sides. Drain well. Place bean curd between absorbent kitchen towels and gently press out excess oil.
4. Slice each bean curd into 9 cubes and arrange on a large serving plate or individual serving plates.
5. Ladle peanut sauce over and garnish with bean sprouts and cucumber strips. Serve hot.

APPETISERS & LIGHT MEALS 43

SAMOSA DAGING BEREMPAH

Makes 25–30 pieces

This triangular-shaped stuffed pastry is a popular snack among the Indian community. It consists of a thick pastry crust filled with spiced potatoes, onions, peas, coriander and lentils. My mother made some modifications to this afternoon snack, resulting in samosas that are made using strips of spring roll skin, with a flavourful filling consisting mainly of spicy ground beef, onions and coriander leaves. The samosas are deep-fried until crispy and golden brown and often served hot with a specially-made sweet chilli sauce.

Spring roll skins 60 large sheets, about 20 x 20-cm (8 x 8-in), thawed
Plain (all-purpose) flour 5 Tbsp, mixed with a little water into a thick paste
Vegetable oil as needed

Filling
Ginger 2.5-cm (1-in) knob, peeled and sliced
Garlic 3 cloves, peeled
Minced beef 250 g (9 oz)
Ground white pepper 1 tsp
Soup spices powder (*rempah sup*) 1 Tbsp
Onions 3, peeled and diced
Coriander leaves (cilantro) 2 sprigs
Salt to taste

Chilli Sauce
Red chillies 6–7, seeded
Garlic 7 cloves, peeled
Water 250 ml (8 fl oz / 1 cup)
Tomato ketchup 2 Tbsp
White vinegar or lemon juice 1 Tbsp
Sugar 2 Tbsp
Salt to taste

APPETISERS & LIGHT MEALS 45

1. Prepare filling. Using a blender, process ginger and garlic into a paste.
2. Heat some oil in a non-stick pan over medium heat. Add ginger-garlic paste and stir-fry until lightly browned.
3. Add minced beef and stir consistently until meat is cooked. Add pepper and soup spices powder and stir until well combined.
4. Add onions and coriander leaves and mix well. Season to taste with salt. Cook for a further 5 minutes before removing from heat. Set aside to drain and cool. Filling has to be well drained to ensure samosas are crisp.
5. In the meantime, prepare chilli sauce if desired. Combine chillies and garlic in a blender and process into a paste. In a medium saucepan, gently stir paste with water over medium heat until it simmers. Do not bring to the boil. Remove from heat and stir in tomato ketchup, vinegar and sugar. Season with salt to taste. Set aside while preparing samosas.
6. Prepare spring roll skins. Without peeling skins apart, cut skins into 3 equal strips. Cover with a damp cloth to keep skins moist.
7. To make a samosa, peel off 2 strips of spring roll skins, keeping them stuck together.
8. Fold the bottom left corner up towards the middle of the long edge on the right. Bring the folded skin up so it forms an equilateral triangle and a pocket for the filling.
9. Spoon some filling into the pocket, ensuring that the corners are filled as well. Fold filled pocket up to enclose filling, then brush skin with some flour paste to seal samosa.
10. Repeat procedure until filling is used up.
11. Heat enough oil for deep-frying over medium-high heat. Deep-fry samosas in batches until golden brown and crispy. Drain well and serve warm.

NOTE

- Soup spices powder can be substituted with briyani or curry powder.
- Using two layers of skin per samosa makes for a crunchier, crispier product.
- Be sure to completely seal the samosas while folding to prevent oil from seeping into the pastry while frying.

APPETISERS & LIGHT MEALS

RICE & NOODLES

Nasi Lemak & Sambal Tumis Ikan Bilis 50
Nasi Ayam 54
Lontong Sayur Lodeh 58
Nasi Goreng Kampung Cili Hijau 60
Nasi Pulau 62
Nasi Jagung 64
Pulut Kuning 66
Soto Ayam 68
Roti Kirai 70
Mee Rebus 72
Laksa Johor Nani 76
Mee Telur Daging 78

NASI LEMAK & SAMBAL TUMIS IKAN BILIS

Serves 5–6

Nasi lemak is often served for breakfast, although it is now also prepared for other meals throughout the day. It was traditionally wrapped in banana leaves and accompanied with fried anchovies, fried peanuts, cucumber slices, omelette and spicy *sambal*. These days, *nasi lemak* may also be accompanied with *ayam goreng berempah* (page 36). In our household, our mother served *nasi lemak* with *sambal tumis ikan bilis*, sunny side up eggs, *kangkong belacan* (page 126), fried fish and/or fried chicken.

Long grain rice 640 g (1 lb 7 oz), rinsed and drained
Coconut milk 400 ml (13 1/3 fl oz)
Water 240 ml (8 fl oz / 1 cup)
Salt 1/2 Tbsp or to taste
Vegetable oil as needed
Pandan leaves 3, tied into a knot

Sambal Tumis Ikan Bilis

Garlic 5 cloves, peeled
Dried chillies 15–20, according to taste, soaked in water to soften, then cut into short lengths
Dried prawn (shrimp) paste (*belacan*) 20 g (2/3 oz)
Onions 3, peeled and sliced
Vegetable oil 2 Tbsp
Dried anchovies 200 g (7 oz)
Tamarind pulp 30 g (1 oz), mixed with 6 Tbsp water and strained
Salt to taste
Sugar 1 Tbsp or to taste

Accompaniments

Eggs 5–6
Raw skinned peanuts 100 g (3 1/2 oz)
Cucumber 1, peeled and sliced

1. Prepare rice. Using a rice cooker, combine rice with coconut milk and water. Add salt and 2 Tbsp oil. Stir well. Submerge pandan leaves in pot and leave rice to cook. When rice is cooked, use a rice paddle to stir rice so the flavours are well mixed. Keep warm.

2. Prepare *sambal tumis ikan bilis*. Combine garlic, dried chillies, dried prawn paste and 2 sliced onions in a blender. Process into a paste.

3. Heat some oil in a frying pan. Add dried anchovies and fry lightly. Drain well. Set half the anchovies aside for serving plain.

4. Reheat pan with some oil. Add ground paste and cook over low heat for 20–30 minutes, stirring occasionally.

5. Add tamarind juice and season to taste with salt and sugar. Toss in balance of sliced onion and cook for a further 10 minutes. Return half the fried anchovies to pan. If mixture is too dry, add a small amount of water and simmer over low heat until mixture thickens. Set aside to cool.

6. Prepare accompaniments. Heat some oil in a frying pan and cook eggs individually, sunny side up. Set aside.

7. Preheat oven to 190°C (370°F) and bake peanuts for 10–15 minutes or until lightly browned. Alternatively, heat some oil in a frying pan over medium-high heat. Fry peanuts until lightly browned. Drain well and set aside.

8. Serve rice with *sambal tumis ikan bilis,* fried anchovies and eggs. If desired, serve with additional accompaniments such as *ayam goreng berempah* (page 36) and *kangkong belacan* (page 126).

NOTE

- *Nasi lemak* is traditionally served with the suggested accompaniments and wrapped in banana leaves to enhance its flavour.
- To prepare fried fish, coat several small horse mackerel with a pinch of salt and some ground turmeric mixed with some water. Leave to stand for 15 minutes before deep-frying until golden brown and crisp.

RICE & NOODLES 53

NASI AYAM

Serves 5–6

Chicken rice, particularly when prepared the Hainanese way, is often recognised as a traditionally Chinese dish. The Malays have adapted the popular dish into *nasi ayam*, often replacing the roasted or steamed chicken with fried chicken. My mother's original marinade churns out fried chicken that adds to the rich flavour of the rice. When cooked to perfection, the chicken is crispy on the outside and juicy on the inside. My sisters and I also love the Chinese-inspired *chap chye* (page 128) that our mother used to serve with *nasi ayam*.

Chicken Stock and Soup
Chicken 1 thigh
Water 2 litres (64 fl oz / 8 cups)
Chicken stock cube 1
Garlic 5 cloves, peeled and bruised
Ground white pepper 1 tsp
Salt to taste

Rice
Vegetable oil as needed
Garlic 9 cloves, peeled and sliced
Ginger 5-cm (2-in) knob, peeled and sliced
Long grain rice 800 g (1^3/$_4$ lb), rinsed and drained
Sesame oil 2 Tbsp
Salt 1 tsp
Pandan leaves 3, tied into a knot

Fried Chicken
Dried chillies 10, soaked to soften, then cut into short lengths
Garlic 7 cloves, peeled
Ground turmeric 1^1/$_2$ tsp
Coarse salt 1 tsp
Chicken parts (chicken legs often turn out juicier) 1 kg (2 lb 3 oz)
Vegetable oil for deep-frying

Chilli Sauce
Red chillies 6
Red bird's eye chillies 5
Ginger 1-cm (^{1}/$_2$-in) knob, peeled and sliced
Garlic 3 cloves, peeled and chopped
Salt 1 tsp or to taste
Sugar 1 Tbsp or to taste
Limes 2, juice extracted

Accompaniments
Tomatoes 2, sliced
Cucumber 1, sliced
Lettuce a few leaves

1. Prepare chicken stock. Boil chicken thigh with water and chicken stock cube for about 15 minutes or until some oil has begun to surface. Set aside.

2. In a heavy saucepan over medium heat, stir-fry bruised garlic until lightly browned and fragrant. Scoop some chicken stock (sufficient for serving as soup) and add to garlic in pan. Season with pepper and salt to taste.

3. Set aside chicken soup. When ready to serve, garnish with crisp-fried shallots and coriander leaves and spring onions, if desired.

4. Prepare rice. Heat some oil in a saucepan over medium heat. Add garlic and ginger and stir-fry until lightly browned.

5. Transfer browned garlic and ginger to a rice cooker pot. Add rice and sesame oil. Stir for 2–3 minutes.

6. Measure out 800 ml ($26^{2}/_{3}$ fl oz) chicken stock prepared earlier and add to rice cooker pot. Add salt and submerge pandan leaves in pot. Mix well and leave rice to cook.

7. Prepare marinade for fried chicken. Combine dried chillies, garlic, ground turmeric and salt in a blender and process into a smooth paste. Spoon paste on chicken and mix well. Leave to marinate for about 30 minutes.

8. Heat oil in a frying pan and deep-fry chicken in batches until cooked and browned. Drain well and set aside.

9. Prepare chilli sauce. Combine chillies, ginger and garlic in a blender and process into a paste. In a medium saucepan, gently stir ground paste with salt, sugar and lime juice and bring to the boil. Set aside to cool before serving.

10. Serve rice with fried chicken, sliced cucumber, sliced tomato, lettuce and chicken soup. Offer chilli sauce on the side.

Photograph on page 56

LONTONG SAYUR LODEH

Serves 4–6

Lontong is compressed rice. It can be served with dishes such as *sate ayam* (page 34) and *soto ayam* (page 68). It is also most frequently served with *sayur lodeh*, a broth with lots of vegetables. What is interesting about *lontong sayur lodeh* is that this dish is commonly served as breakfast as well as on special occasions such as Eid. During Eid, a more substantive version of *lontong* is served with accompaniments such as *bergedil* (page 108), *sambal tumis udang* (page 94), *serunding daging* (page 110), *rendang daging* (page 104), *sambal goreng* (page 112) and *kari ayam Melayu* (page 116).

Vegetable oil as needed

Tempeh 2 pieces, sliced on the diagonal

Fried firm bean curd 3 pieces, halved into triangles

Prawns (shrimps) 10, medium, peeled and deveined, leaving tails intact

Lemon grass 2 stalks, ends trimmed

Bay leaves 5

Red and green chillies 2 each, slit midway

Galangal 5-cm (2-in) knob, peeled

Turmeric leaf 1

Kaffir lime leaves 5

Water as needed

Jicama 1/2, small, peeled and thinly sliced into 3-cm (1-in) lengths

Carrot 1, small, peeled and cut to 2.5-cm (1-in) lengths

Long beans 4, cut to 2.5-cm (1-in) lengths

White cabbage 1/2, medium, sliced

Slender aubergine (eggplant/brinjal) 1, cut into 0.5-cm (1/4-in) thick slices

Coconut milk 400 ml (13 1/3 fl oz)

Salt to taste

Sugar to taste

Crisp-fried shallots 2 Tbsp

Spice Paste

Onions 2, peeled

Garlic 5 cloves, peeled

Coriander seeds 1 Tbsp, soaked for 10 minutes; drained before use

Cumin seeds 1/2 Tbsp, soaked for 10 minutes; drained before use

Fennel seeds 1/2 Tbsp, soaked for 10 minutes; drained before use

Dried prawns (shrimps) 50 g (1 2/3 oz), soaked for 10 minutes; drained before use

Dried prawn (shrimp) paste (*belacan*) 20 g (2/3 oz)

Dried anchovies 30 g (1 oz), soaked for 10 minutes; drained before use

Dried chillies 10, soaked to soften, then cut into short lengths

Turmeric 2.5-cm (1-in) knob, peeled

1. Heat some oil in a frying pan and fry tempeh until lightly browned. Drain well and set aside.
2. Add more oil and reheat. Fry bean curd until lightly browned. Drain well and set aside.
3. Prepare spice paste. Combine all ingredients in a blender and process into a paste.
4. In a heavy saucepan, heat 5 Tbsp oil over medium heat. Add spice paste and stir-fry until lightly browned and fragrant.
5. Add prawns and briefly stir-fry. Add lemon grass, bay leaves, chillies, galangal, turmeric leaf and kaffir lime leaves. Add a little water to help with stir-frying. Cook until fragrant.
6. Add more water to adjust gravy to desired thickness, then add jicama, carrot and long beans and mix well. After about a minute, add cabbage, aubergine, fried tempeh and fried firm bean curd. Boil for about 10 minutes.
7. Stir in coconut milk and simmer over low heat, stirring consistently.
8. Season with salt and sugar to taste.
9. Dish out and garnish with crisp-fried shallots. Serve with *lontong* (page 31).

NOTE
- Ready-made *lontong* is available from some supermarkets.

Photograph on page 57

NASI GORENG KAMPUNG CILI HIJAU

Serves 5–6

Nasi Goreng is a very popular rice dish and perhaps, as a result, there are now many ways to prepare it. It is commonly cooked using leftover rice. Typically, you can mix this dish up with almost any kind of meat, egg and vegetables. Serve with fried chicken or skewers of *sate* (page 34) and prawn crackers on the side.

Plain rice 480 g (1 lb 1 oz), cooled
Vegetable oil 4 Tbsp
Eggs 4, beaten
Coriander leaves (cilantro) 10 g ($1/3$ oz), sliced
Spring onions (scallions) 10 g ($1/3$ oz), sliced
Salt to taste

Ground Paste
Dried prawns (shrimps) 100 g ($3^1/_2$ oz), soaked for 10 minutes; drained before use
Dried anchovies 50 g ($1^2/_3$ oz)
Green chillies 4
Red chilli 1
Red bird's eye chillies 5
Onions 2, peeled and chopped
Garlic 6 cloves, peeled

Garnish & Accompaniments
Crisp-fried shallots as desired
Fried anchovies (page 51) as desired
Prawn crackers as desired

1. Prepare ground paste. Using a mortar and pestle, grind soaked dried prawns and dried anchovies. Set aside. Grind rest of ingredients separately, then mix with dried prawns and dried anchovies until well combined. (Alternatively, combine all ingredients in a blender and process into a coarse paste).

2. Heat oil in a wok over medium heat. Add ground paste and stir-fry until lightly browned and fragrant.

3. Add eggs a quarter at a time until well combined with paste. Leave eggs to cook for a few minutes before adding rice. Add rice and fry for a few minutes until ingredients are well mixed. Season to taste with salt.

4. Toss in coriander leaves and spring onions. Fry for another minute before removing from heat.

5. Garnish with crisp-fried shallots and sprinkle over some fried anchovies. Offer some prawn crackers on the side.

NOTE

- The ground paste will be more flavourful when ground using a mortar and pestle instead of a blender as the paste should be coarse and not too fine.
- Adjust the number of chillies used according to taste.

RICE & NOODLES 61

NASI PULAU

Serves 5–6

Unlike most rice dishes in Malay cooking, the beef in *nasi pulau* is cooked together with the rice. The juices from the beef adds another dimension of flavour to the rice, giving *nasi pulau* a unique taste. The highlight of this dish is the special chilli sauce that accompanies it. The sauce complements the richness of the rice with a tinge of spiciness—a perfect combination of tastes. This version of *nasi pulau* was introduced to my mother by my mother-in-law, Shariffah Suhailah Alhady. It was the signature dish of my late sister-in-law, Shariffa Zubaidah. My mother and mother-in-law used to openly share the recipes of their signature dishes with each other. I was inspired by their willingness to continually learn from and share with other great cooks. These ladies clearly believed that recipes should be shared.

Vegetable oil 4–5 Tbsp

Long grain rice 500 g (1 lb 1$^1/_2$ oz), rinsed and drained

Salt to taste

Beef Stock

Beef short ribs 500 g (1 lb 1$^1/_2$ oz), cut into 5-cm (2-in) lengths

Water 500 ml (16 fl oz / 2 cups)

Garlic 10–12 cloves, left unpeeled, but cleaned and bruised

Onions 2, peeled and sliced

Coriander seeds 2 Tbsp

Cumin seeds 1 tsp

Fennel seeds 1 tsp

Cinnamon 1 stick

Ginger 5-cm (2-in) knob, peeled and thinly sliced

Chilli Sauce

Dried chillies 15, soaked to soften and cut into short lengths

Tamarind pulp 40 g (1$^1/_3$ oz), mixed with 3$^1/_2$ Tbsp water and strained

Palm sugar (*gula melaka*) 100 g (3$^1/_2$ oz), grated

Salt to taste

Onion 1, peeled and thinly sliced

1. Prepare beef stock. In a heavy saucepan, combine all ingredients for beef stock and boil for about 20 minutes or until meat is tender. Using a strainer, scoop up meat and cut into pieces. Set aside. Scoop up all other ingredients and set aside. Set beef stock aside.
2. Heat oil in a wok over medium heat. Cook meat further by stir-frying for 3–5 minutes or until meat is lightly browned. Drain and set aside.
3. Reheat wok and add other ingredients scooped up from beef stock. Stir-fry until fragrant. Drain and set aside.
4. Place rice and beef stock in a rice cooker. Be sure that the amount of liquid to rice is equal. Toss in stir-fried beef and stock ingredients. Add salt to taste. Leave rice to cook.
5. Prepare chilli sauce. Boil a small pot of water and add dried chillies. Boil for about 10 minutes, then drain. Grind boiled dried chillies with some water. Place in a bowl with tamarind juice, palm sugar and salt. Mix until well combined. Toss sliced onion into chilli sauce only when ready to serve.
6. Serve rice warm with chilli sauce on the side.

NASI JAGUNG

Serves 5–6

Corn adds a tinge of sweetness to this buttery rice dish typically served with *sambal tumis udang* (page 94), *kurma ayam* (page 114) or *ayam masak merah* (page 118). *Nasi jagung* is increasingly served at weddings as an alternative to the traditional *nasi minyak* or *nasi briyani*. *Nasi jagung* is also a favourite at my family gatherings. My mother would cook it to commemorate special occasions and invite family and friends over.

Long grain rice 500 g (1 lb 1½ oz), rinsed and drained
Water as needed
Ground turmeric a pinch
Butter 2 Tbsp
Onion 1, peeled and thinly sliced
Cloves 3
Cardamoms 3
Star anise 1
Cinnamon 1 stick
Evaporated milk 100 ml (3½ fl oz)

Salt to taste
Pandan leaves 3, tied into a knot
Sweet corn 1 ear, husked and kernels sliced
Coriander leaves (cilantro) 4 sprigs

Ground Paste
Garlic 4 cloves, peeled
Onions 2, peeled
Ginger 2.5-cm (1-in) knob, peeled and thinly sliced

1. In a basin, soak rice in some water mixed with ground turmeric (for colouring). Leave for at least 30 minutes. Drain before using.
2. Prepare ground paste. Combine garlic, onions and ginger in a blender and process into a paste. Set aside.
3. Heat butter in a large saucepan. Add onion and stir-fry until lightly browned and fragrant. Add cloves, cardamoms, star anise, cinnamon and ground paste. Stir until well combined.
4. Add 500 ml (16 fl oz / 2 cups) water and boil for about 5 minutes.
5. Transfer mixture to a rice cooker. Add evaporated milk, salt to taste and drained soaked rice. Submerge pandan leaves in rice and leave rice to cook.
6. When rice is about three-quarter way done, sprinkle corn kernels into rice and stir gently. Leave rice to continue cooking. When rice is done, add coriander leaves.
7. Serve hot with *sambal tumis udang* (page 94), *kurma ayam* (page 114) or *ayam masak merah* (page 118) and *paceri nenas* (page 134).

NOTE

- Soaking the rice before cooking will ensure that the rice is tender and not hard when cooked.

PULUT KUNING

Serves 4–5

Traditionally, *pulut kuning* is as indispensable as cake is on celebratory occasions such as birthdays and religious observations. This glutinous rice dish is often served with *rendang daging* (page 104) or *kari ayam Melayu* (page 116) and *sambal tumis udang* (page 94). In recent years, a return to tradition has been observed in Malay weddings with wedding cakes being replaced with tiered *pulut kuning*. These are often presented with elaborate garnishes for outstanding visual appeal. My mother would cook *pulut kuning* to acknowledge very special occasions such as when any of us completed reading the Quran (*qatam* Quran) or when we did well in our school examinations.

Glutinous rice 500 g (1 lb 1½ oz)
Water as needed
Ground turmeric 1 Tbsp
Eggs 2
Coconut milk 250 ml (8 fl oz / 1 cup)
Salt 1 tsp or to taste
Pandan leaves 3, tied into a knot
Banana leaves 3 sheets
Red chilli 1, sliced

1. In a basin, soak rice in some water mixed with ground turmeric (for colouring). Leave for at least 30 minutes. Drain before using.
2. Prepare eggs. They can either be cooked into omelettes, then rolled up and sliced or hard-boiled. Set aside.
3. Place rice into a steaming bowl. Steam rice for about 15 minutes or until half cooked. Remove from heat.
4. In a bowl, mix coconut milk with salt, then stir evenly into rice. Return rice to steamer and continue steaming until rice is cooked and tender.
5. Scoop steamed rice onto a tray and press lightly using banana leaves into desired shape. Allow to cool.
6. Garnish with sliced red chillies. Serve with *rendang daging* (page 104), *sambal tumis udang* (page 94) and egg rolls or hard-boiled eggs.

RICE & NOODLES 67

SOTO AYAM

Serves 4–5

This shredded chicken soup with *lontong* is served with *bergedil* (page 108) and garnished with bean sprouts and crisp-fried shallots. *Soto ayam* is also never complete without its special, spicy bird's eye chilli sauce—just a dash will usually suffice, for the chilli may be overwhelming at first taste.

Vegetable oil as needed
Soup spices powder (*rempah sup*) 2 Tbsp
Lemon grass 2 stalks, ends trimmed and bruised
Kaffir lime leaves 7
Water as needed
Salt to taste
Bean sprouts 200 g (7 oz), blanched

Basic Chicken Stock
Chicken 1, medium, cut into 4 pieces
Water 1.5 litres (48 fl oz / 6 cups)

Spice Paste
Shallots 12, peeled
Garlic 7 cloves, peeled
Galangal 5-cm (2-in) knob, peeled
Ginger 5-cm (2-in) knob, peeled
Candlenuts 4
Coriander seeds 2 Tbsp
Cumin seeds 1 Tbsp, soaked for 10 minutes; drained before use
Fennel seeds 1 Tbsp, soaked for 10 minutes; drained before use

Bird's Eye Chilli Sauce
Red bird's eye chillies 15
Sweet soy sauce 7 Tbsp
Garlic 3 cloves, peeled
Sugar 2 Tbsp
Salt to taste

Accompaniments
Lontong (page 31) as desired
Fine rice vermicelli (optional) as desired, blanched
Bergedil (page 108) as desired

Garnish
Crisp-fried shallots as desired
Coriander leaves (cilantro) as desired
Spring onions (scallions) as desired

1. Prepare basic chicken stock, boil chicken with water in a pot for about 20 minutes.
2. Prepare spice paste. Put all ingredients in a blender and process into a paste. Heat some oil in a heavy saucepan over medium heat. Add spice paste and stir-fry until lightly browned and fragrant.
3. Add soup spices powder and mix well. Add bruised lemon grass and kaffir lime leaves. Add some water and stir until spice paste is well mixed with water.
4. Pour mixture into basic chicken stock to make soup. Season with salt to taste. Bring to the boil.
5. Remove chicken from soup. Leave to cool slightly before shredding meat. Keep soup warm.
6. Prepare bird's eye chilli sauce. Combine bird's eye chillies, sweet soy sauce, garlic and sugar in a blender and process into a paste. Transfer to a small bowl and season with salt to taste.
7. To serve, place *lontong* (page 31) and/or rice vermicelli in individual serving bowls or deep dishes. Top with shredded chicken and ladle soup over. Serve with *bergedil* (page 108) and bird's eye chilli sauce on the side. Garnish with crisp-fried shallots, coriander and spring onions.

ROTI KIRAI

Serves 6–8

This Malay crêpe is also known as *roti jala*, literally translated as net bread. Handling the special ladle for making these crêpes can be a challenge at the first attempt, but it only gets easier. My youngest sister, Rita Zuhaida, recalled that she had her first go at making these crêpes when she was about seven years old. Our mother was a perfectionist. She would insist that the crêpes are not made too thick, too thin or fried too crispy. In our household, *roti kirai* is often served with *kari ayam Melayu* (page 116) and egg salad and topped with its special spicy chilli sauce. Best served when warm, *roti kirai* remains one of our family's favourites for weekend meals, breaking fast during Ramadhan and small home parties.

Yellow food colouring 1 tsp
Ghee 1 Tbsp, for brushing
Pandan leaves 3, tied into a knot to be used as a brush

Crêpe Batter
Plain (all-purpose) flour 500 g (1 lb 1 1/2 oz)
Rice flour 1 Tbsp
Eggs 2, beaten
Evaporated milk 200 ml (7 fl oz)
Water 1 litre (32 fl oz / 4 cups) + 4 Tbsp
Salt 1 tsp or to taste

Chilli Sauce
Vegetable oil as needed
Raw skinned peanuts 100 g (3 1/2 oz)
Red chillies 6
Ginger 1-cm (1/2-in) knob, peeled and sliced
Garlic 3 cloves, peeled and chopped
Sugar 1 Tbsp
Salt to taste
Tomato ketchup 2 Tbsp

Accompaniments
Lettuce as desired
Tomatoes as desired
Hard-boiled eggs as desired

1. Prepare crêpe batter. Combine all ingredients in an electric blender. Test that batter is the right consistency using *roti kirai* mould. It should flow easily. If it is too thick, adjust with some water. Mix well.
2. Sift batter to remove any lumps. Add yellow food colouring and stir well until mixture is evenly coloured. Let batter stand for 5 minutes before using.
3. Heat a large frying pan and coat lightly with ghee using pandan brush. Scoop batter using *roti kirai* mould and form crêpes by moving mould over pan in a circular motion. When crêpe is lightly set, brush lightly with ghee.
4. Fold crêpe into a wedge and set aside on a serving plate. Repeat until batter is used up.
5. Prepare chilli sauce. Heat some oil in a frying pan and fry peanuts until lightly browned. Drain well and leave to cool. Using a food chopper, grind cooled fried peanuts coarsely.
6. Place other ingredients except tomato ketchup for chilli sauce in a blender and process. Transfer to a bowl and mix well with ground peanuts. Gently stir in tomato ketchup until sauce is well combined.
7. Serve *roti kirai* with *kari ayam Melayu* (page 116), lettuce, tomatoes and hard-boiled eggs and chilli sauce on the side.

MEE REBUS

Serves 4–6

Mee rebus is a perfect example of infusing elements of other immigrant groups into a Malay dish. Some versions of the dish, like our mother's, include beef as an ingredient. Often served as breakfast, *mee rebus* is garnished with hard-boiled eggs, limes, green chillies, fried bean curd, crisp-fried shallots, spring onions and bean sprouts. *Mee rebus*, alongside *tahu goreng* (page 42), *sate ayam* (page 34), *rojak, air bandung soda* (page 172) and *goreng pisang* are among the standard dishes my parents would prepare whenever they set up food booths at fun fairs, carnivals and charity events.

Beef (include fatty parts) 150 g (5 1/3 oz), cut into cubes and boiled in 2 litres (64 fl oz / 8 cups) water or as much water required to make gravy

Prawns (shrimps) 10, peeled and deveined, leaving tails intact

Vegetable oil as needed

Onion 1, peeled and sliced

Beef curry powder 2 Tbsp

Preserved soy bean paste 2 Tbsp, rinsed and drained

Raw skinned peanuts 80 g (2 4/5 oz), fried and ground

Sweet potatoes 2, medium, boiled, peeled and mashed

Plain (all-purpose) flour 2 Tbsp

Salt to taste

Sugar to taste

Hokkien noodles 500 g (1 lb 1 1/2 oz), blanched and drained

Sweet soy sauce (optional) to taste

Ground Paste

Onions 2, peeled and chopped

Garlic 7 cloves, peeled

Dried prawns (shrimps) 80 g (2 4/5 oz), soaked for 10 minutes; drained before use

Dried chillies 10, soaked to soften, then cut into short lengths

Ginger 5-cm (2-in) knob, peeled and sliced

Dried prawn (shrimp) paste (*belacan*) 20 g (2/3 oz)

Garnish

Bean sprouts 50 g (1 2/3 oz), blanched and drained

Fried bean curd 2 pieces, cut into small cubes and fried

Hard-boiled eggs 4, peeled and sliced

Green chillies 4, sliced

Coriander leaves (cilantro) as desired, chopped

Spring onions (scallions) as desired, chopped

Crisp-fried shallots as desired

1. Prepare beef stock. Boil 2 litres (64 fl oz / 8 cups) water in a heavy saucepan. Add beef and lower heat to simmer for about 20 minutes or until beef is tender. Using a strainer, scoop up meat and cut into pieces. Return meat to beef stock. Set aside.

2. In another pan, boil 450 ml (15 fl oz) water and boil prawns until they change colour and are cooked. Drain prawns and set aside. Measure out 470 ml ($15^{2}/_{3}$ fl oz) prawn stock. Set aside.

3. Prepare ground paste. Combine all ingredients in a blender and process into a paste.

4. Heat some oil in a heavy saucepan and add sliced onion. Stir-fry until lightly browned and fragrant. Add ground paste and repeat to stir-fry until lightly browned and fragrant.

5. Add beef curry powder, stirring continuously, then add prawn stock, prawns and beef stock together with sliced beef. Stir in preserved soy bean paste, ground peanuts and mashed sweet potatoes. Bring to the boil.

6. Stir in flour to thicken gravy. Season with salt and sugar to taste.

7. To serve, put some Hokkien noodles and bean sprouts into individual serving bowls or deep dishes. Ladle hot gravy over. Garnish with fried bean curd, hard-boiled eggs, green chillies, coriander leaves, spring onions and crisp-fried shallots.

8. For additional flavour, drizzle with sweet soy sauce. Serve immediately.

Photograph on page 74

RICE & NOODLES 75

LAKSA JOHOR NANI

Serves 5–7

There are generally two basic types of laksa: *laksa lemak*, noodles in coconut curry soup and *asam laksa*, a fragrant Penang version with a distinctive fishy flavour. My mother's version is called *laksa Johor*, an authentic recipe from Johor where she was from, and it is my husband's favourite dish. We call this dish *laksa Johor nani* after my mother as *nani* means maternal grandmother in Hindi and that is what her grandchildren called her. My daughter, Sharifah Nadhrah, particularly loves this laksa as my mother used to thrill her grandchildren by incorporating contemporary accompaniments they liked such as fishcake and fried bean curd into the dish. Therefore, *laksa Johor nani* is rather unique. It plays off smooth laksa noodles against a rich, velvety gravy, topped with bean sprouts, fishcakes, fried bean curd, laksa leaves and special chilli paste on the side.

Vegetable oil as needed
Water about 1 litre (32 fl oz / 4 cups)
Coconut milk 300 ml (10 fl oz / 1¼ cups)
Salt to taste
Fresh laksa noodles 500 g (1 lb 1½ oz), blanched

Ground Paste
Wolf herring 100 g (3½ oz)
Dried prawns (shrimps) 50 g (1⅔ oz), soaked for 10 minutes; drained before use
Dried chillies 10, soaked to soften, then cut into short lengths
Onions 2, peeled and chopped
Garlic 5 cloves, peeled
Lemon grass 2 stalks, ends trimmed and cut into short lengths
Galangal 2.5-cm (1-in) knob, peeled
Fish curry powder 1½ Tbsp

Chilli Sauce
Dried prawn (shrimp) paste (*belacan*) 20 g (⅔ oz)
Red chillies 5
Red bird's eye chillies 5
Salt to taste
Sugar to taste

Accompaniments
Bean sprouts 50 g (1⅔ oz), blanched
Laksa leaves 50 g (1⅔ oz), thinly sliced
Fishcakes 3 large pieces or about 300 g (11 oz), fried and sliced
Fried bean curd puffs 14 pieces, sliced in half

1. Prepare fish and dried prawns for ground paste. Boil a pot of water and add fish. Boil until fish is cooked. Drain and leave to cool. Remove and discard fish bones. Using a mortar and pestle, pound fish. Set aside. Repeat to pound soaked dried prawns. Set aside.

2. Place all other ingredients for ground paste into a blender and process into a paste.

3. In a heavy saucepan, heat some oil and add ground paste. Stir-fry until fragrant, then add ground fish and dried prawns. Lower heat to a simmer.

4. Stir in water and coconut milk to make gravy. Stir until heated through. Season with salt and sugar to taste. Keep gravy at a simmer.

5. Prepare dried prawn paste for chilli sauce. In a small frying pan, dry-roast dried prawn paste for a few minutes until fragrant. Place roasted prawn paste and chillies in a blender and process into a paste. Season with salt and sugar to taste.

6. To serve, place noodles in individual serving bowls or deep dishes. Ladle some hot gravy over noodles and top with desired accompaniments. Serve with chilli sauce on the side.

NOTE

- If laksa noodles are not available, spaghetti can be used as a substitute.

Photograph on page 75

MEE TELUR DAGING

Serves 4–6

This spicy beef noodle dish is another interesting combination of cross-ethnic elements—Hokkien noodles from the Chinese and thick and spicy curry-like gravy from the Indians. The semi-cooked egg that accompanies the noodles adds a special flavour to the rich taste of the gravy. This satisfying dish can be served at any time of the day.

Vegetable oil as needed
Garlic 5 cloves, peeled and finely chopped
Onion 1, peeled and thinly sliced
Beef 300 g (11 oz), cut into cubes
Water 400 ml (13 1/3 fl oz)
Tomato ketchup 125 ml (4 fl oz / 1/2 cup)
Light soy sauce 100 ml (3 1/2 fl oz)
Sweet soy sauce 5 Tbsp
Sugar to taste

Eggs 4–6
Chinese flowering cabbage 3 stalks
Hokkien noodles 500 g (1 lb 1 1/2 oz), blanched
Crisp-fried shallots (optional) to taste

Ground Paste

Dried chillies 15, soaked to soften, then cut into short lengths
Onion 1, peeled and thinly sliced

1. Prepare ground paste. Place dried chillies and onion in a blender and process into a paste.
2. Heat some oil in a wok over medium heat. Add garlic and onion and stir-fry until lightly browned and fragrant. Add ground paste. Continue to stir-fry.
3. Add beef and stir-fry until meat is thoroughly cooked and tender. Add some water to help with stirring the mixture. Continue to stir.
4. Add tomato ketchup, light soy sauce and sweet soy sauce. Season with sugar to taste. Bring to the boil. Add more water to achieve desired thickness of gravy. Stir well until combined.
5. To prepare a single serving, ladle 8 Tbsp gravy into a small pot. Stir in some water to adjust thickness as desired and bring to the boil. Add an egg. Leave for a minute to poach egg.
6. Add Chinese flowering cabbage. Place some blanched noodles into individual serving bowls or deep dishes and pour gravy over. Garnish with crisp-fried shallots.
7. Repeat to prepare desired number of servings.

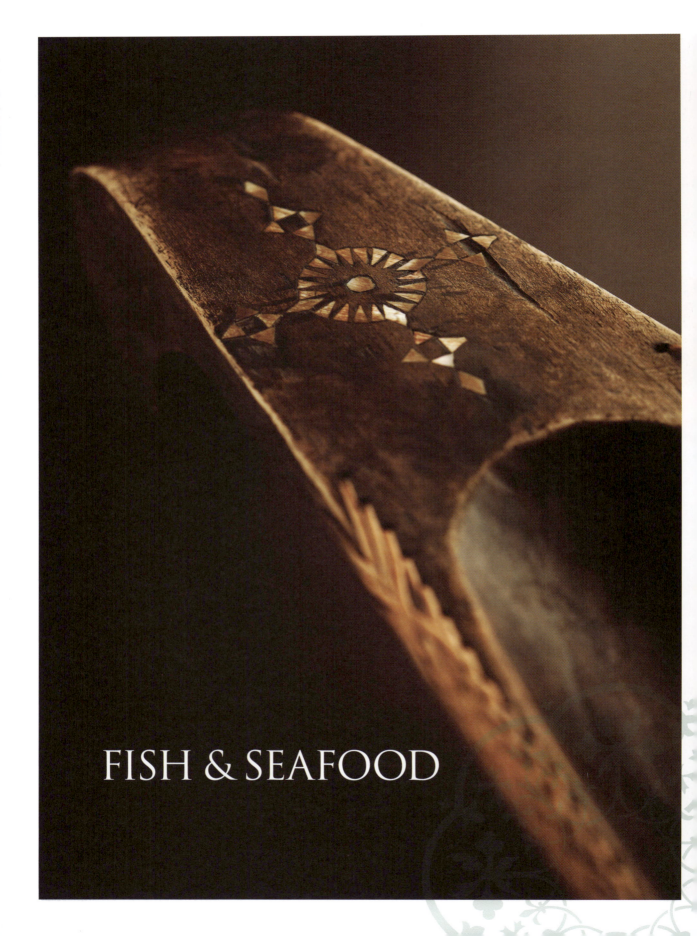

FISH & SEAFOOD

Asam Pedas Ikan 82

Ikan Sumbat Berlada 84

Ikan Goreng Masam Manis 86

Ikan Bungkus Daun Pisang 88

Ketam Masak Lemak Cili Padi 90

Udang Bakar 92

Sambal Tumis Udang 94

Sambal Sotong Daging Sumbat 96

ASAM PEDAS IKAN

Serves 5–7

The taste of this spicy, tamarind fish stew is wonderfully complex. It combines the spiciness of chilli with the sourness of tamarind. The taste is further enhanced by the juiciness of the fish and the crunchiness of the vegetables. *Asam pedas ikan* is a very common dish in Malay households. When we were growing up, my sisters and I would look forward to having our mother's *asam pedas ikan* after a long day in school. Now, as mothers, we serve this to our own children. My mother's *asam pedas ikan* tastes even better if left to sit for a day. We would soak sunny side up eggs in the leftover stew and have it for breakfast with toasted wholemeal bread the next day.

Vegetable oil as needed

Water 700 ml (23$^{1}/_{3}$ fl oz)

Tamarind pulp 100 g (3$^{1}/_{2}$ oz), mixed with 300 ml (10 fl oz / 1$^{1}/_{4}$ cups) water and strained

Lemon grass 1 stalk, ends trimmed and slightly bruised

Stingray 500 g (1 lb 1$^{1}/_{2}$ oz), cut into slices

Laksa leaves 10 stalks

Ladies fingers 5

Salt to taste

Sugar to taste

Ground Paste

Dried chillies 20, soaked to soften, then cut into short lengths

Dried prawn (shrimp) paste (*belacan*) 30 g (1 oz)

Onions 2, peeled and chopped

Garlic 6 cloves, peeled

Turmeric 2.5-cm (1-in) knob, peeled and sliced

Ginger 2.5-cm (1-in) knob, peeled and sliced

1. Prepare ground paste. Combine ingredients for ground paste in a blender and process into a paste.
2. Heat oil in a heavy saucepan over medium heat. Add ground paste and stir-fry until fragrant, stirring continuously to prevent burning.
3. Add water, tamarind juice and lemon grass. When mixture begins to simmer, add stingray. Allow to boil over low heat for about 10 minutes until fish is cooked.
4. Add laksa leaves and ladies fingers. Season with salt and sugar to taste.
5. Dish out and serve hot with plain rice or bread.

NOTE

- Vary the choice of fish used, such as with Spanish mackerel instead of stingray.
- Soak fish slices in some amount of tamarind juice for about 10 minutes to reduce the fishy smell.

IKAN SUMBAT BERLADA

Serves 5–6

Stuffing is a typical style of Malay cooking. Many varieties of seafood, poultry and vegetables are prime candidates for stuffing. Stuffing should be prepared just before using, not in advance. I particularly like this dish of pan-fried Spanish mackerel stuffed with chilli. At first bite, you can immediately taste the flavours of all the different types of leaves and spices used. This is what makes this dish stand out from the other stuffing recipes included in this book.

Vegetable oil as needed

Tamarind pulp 10 g ($1/3$ oz), mixed with 2 Tbsp water and strained

Salt to taste

Sugar to taste

Laksa leaves 20 g ($2/3$ oz), finely sliced

Turmeric leaf 1, finely sliced

Cekur (sand ginger) **leaves** 5, finely sliced

Spanish mackerel 5, medium, cleaned and gutted

Kalamansi limes 2–3, halved

Ground Paste

Dried chillies 15, soaked to soften, then cut into short lengths

Onions 2, peeled and sliced

Garlic 5 cloves, peeled and sliced

Ginger 2.5-cm (1-in) knob, peeled

Lemon grass 2 stalks, ends trimmed and cut into short lengths

Turmeric 2.5-cm (1-in) knob, peeled

1. Prepare ground paste. Combine all ingredients in a blender and process into a paste.
2. Heat some oil in a wok over medium heat. Add ground paste and stir-fry until lightly browned and fragrant.
3. Add tamarind juice and stir-fry for a further 5 minutes. Season with salt and sugar to taste. Add laksa leaves, turmeric leaf and *cekur* leaves. Set aside.
4. Make a slit along the spine of fish to create a pocket for ground paste. Stuff ground paste into fish. Reserve some paste to be spooned over fish when serving.
5. Heat sufficient oil in a wok for frying fish. Lower fish into hot oil and fry until golden brown on one side before turning over to cook the other side. Repeat to cook one fish at a time.
6. Drain well. Arrange fish on a serving plate and spoon reserved ground paste on fish. Serve hot with plain rice. Offer lime halves on the side.

NOTE

- Use a non-stick pan when cooking fish so the fish does not stick to the pan and break up.

IKAN GORENG MASAM MANIS

Serves 4–6

This dish of fried fish in chilli and tomato ketchup has a good mix of sweet and sour tastes. Adapted from the Chinese sweet and sour meat dish, *ikan goreng masam manis* tastefully blends the crispy texture of fried fish with the fluid texture of its accompanying sauce. The taste of this dish not only lies in the sauce but also in the choice of fish. It is best to use firm white fish such as cod, sea bass or halibut. Fish can also be replaced with other kinds of seafood such as prawns (shrimps) or squid.

Vegetable oil for deep-frying
Red snappers 2, large, cleaned and gutted
Egg white from 1 egg, beaten
Salt to taste
Corn flour 100 g (3½ oz)

Sauce
Dried chillies 10, soaked to soften, then cut into short lengths
Garlic 5 cloves, peeled and thinly sliced
Ginger 2.5-cm (1-in) knob, peeled and sliced
Tomato ketchup 7 Tbsp
Chilli sauce 1 Tbsp
Salt to taste
Sugar to taste
Water 450 ml (15 fl oz)
Onion 1, peeled and cut into cubes
Red chillies 4–6, sliced
Green capsicum (bell pepper) 1, medium, cored and seeded, cut into cubes
Canned pineapple rings 100 g (3½ oz), drained, cut into small slices
Corn flour 1 Tbsp, mixed with some water into a paste
Tomato 1, cut into wedges
Crisp-fried shallots 2 Tbsp
Coriander leaves (cilantro) 2 sprigs

1. Prepare sauce. Combine dried chillies and garlic in a blender and process into a paste.
2. Heat some oil in a wok over medium heat. Add paste and stir-fry until fragrant, stirring continuously to prevent burning. Add sliced ginger.
3. Stir in tomato ketchup and chilli sauce. Season with salt and sugar to taste. Add water and continue to stir.
4. Add onion, chillies, capsicum and pineapple. Stir until well combined. Add corn flour paste to thicken sauce. Bring to the boil, then set aside.
5. Marinate fish with egg white and salt. Set aside for 5 minutes.
6. Heat oil for deep-frying. Coat marinated fish with corn flour, then lower into hot oil and fry until fish is golden brown and crispy. Drain well and place on a serving plate.
7. Reheat sauce and add tomato. Bring to the boil. Remove from heat and pour sauce over fish. Garnish with crisp-fried shallots and coriander leaves.

NOTE

- For the fish to be crispy, the oil used for deep-frying must be sufficiently hot before the fish is added to the pan.

IKAN BUNGKUS DAUN PISANG

Serves 6–8

Steaming is one of the best ways to cook fresh fish. Slathered in lots of spices, atypical of Malay cooking, the fish fillets in this dish are wrapped in banana leaves and steamed. You can smell the inviting aroma the moment the banana leaves are peeled open. The combination of the delicate, sweet flavour of the fish and the spices infused into the fish, give this classic dish layers of taste. Nearly any type of fish will work in this recipe, including salmon, red snapper, cod and tilapia. This is a healthy dish that is also easy to cook.

Stingray 500 g (1 lb 1½ oz), cut into desired sizes

Vegetable oil as needed

Dried krill (*udang geragau*) 30 g (1 oz)

Salt to taste

Sugar to taste

Banana leaves as needed, cut into sheets large enough to wrap stingray pieces

Bamboo skewers as needed, cut into 5-cm (2-in) lengths

Kalamansi limes 4–5, halved

Ground Paste

Dried chillies 15, soaked to soften, then cut into short lengths

Onions 2, peeled and sliced

Garlic 5 cloves, peeled and chopped

Lemon grass 2 stalks, ends trimmed and chopped

Candlenuts 3

Galangal 2.5-cm (1-in) knob, peeled and thinly sliced

Ginger 2.5-cm (1-in) knob, peeled and thinly sliced

1. Prepare ground paste. Combine all ingredients in a blender and process into a paste. Marinate stingray with about half the ground paste. Leave to stand for a few minutes.
2. Heat some oil in a wok over medium heat. Add remainder of ground paste and stir-fry until fragrant and lightly brown.
3. Add dried krill and continue to stir. Season with salt and sugar to taste.
4. Place a piece of marinated stingray on a sheet of banana leaf, then coat stingray with some stir-fried ground paste. Wrap stingray with banana leaf and secure parcel using bamboo skewers. Repeat until ingredients are used up.
5. Place parcels in a steamer and steam over medium heat for 20–30 minutes until stingray is tender and cooked.
6. Serve hot with plain rice. Offer kalamansi lime halves on the side.

NOTE

- If banana leaves are unavailable, use aluminium foil.

FISH & SEAFOOD 89

KETAM MASAK LEMAK CILI PADI

Serves 5–6

In Singapore, chilli crab is considered one of the signature seafood dishes of the Chinese community. For the Malays, the equivalent is surely *ketam masak lemak cili padi* or crab in rich, spicy coconut gravy. Crab dishes are an Asian favourite. The sweet juicy flesh within is well worth the hard work needed to de-shell the crab. Paired with a coconut-based gravy, this dish is rich with a tinge of spiciness.

Flower crabs 5, large
Vegetable oil as needed
Lemon grass 2 stalks, ends trimmed and slightly bruised
Galangal 2.5-cm (1-in) knob, peeled and slightly bruised
Kaffir lime leaves 5
Turmeric leaf 1
Water 500 ml (16 fl oz / 2 cups) or more to obtain desired thickness of gravy
Coconut milk 200 ml (7 fl oz)
Salt to taste

Ground Paste
Onions 2, peeled and chopped
Garlic 5 cloves, peeled
Ginger 5-cm (2-in) knob, peeled and chopped
Red bird's eye chillies 10–15
Turmeric 5-cm (2-in) knob, peeled and chopped

1. Place crabs in the freezer for 1 hour. Scrub and wash crabs, then pat dry. Pull off the top hard shell. If there is crab roe, leave it there. Crab roe will add flavour to the dish. Remove and discard feathery gills and membranes from the body. With a sharp cleaver, cut the body in half down its centre. Cut or crack the claws.
2. Prepare ground paste. Combine all ingredients in a blender and process into a paste.
3. Heat some oil in a wok over medium heat. Add ground paste and stir-fry until fragrant and lightly browned.
4. Add lemon grass, galangal, kaffir lime and turmeric leaves and stir-fry. Add some water to help with stirring.
5. When well combined, add remaining water. Bring to the boil, then add coconut milk, stirring continuously.
6. Toss in crabs and season with salt to taste.
7. Dish out and serve hot with plain rice.

NOTE
- Adjust the number of red bird's eye chillies in the ground paste according to your desired level of spiciness for this dish.
- You can substitute the crabs with prawns or lobsters.

UDANG BAKAR

Serves 5–6

My mother was always adventurous in trying out new cooking methods with traditional recipes and this rubbed off on the four of us. My eldest sister loves to experiment with new recipes and instead of the usual oven-baked chicken, she experimented with prawns, coming up with this dish of oven-baked prawns. While some people dislike cooking seafood in the oven because it takes longer, the baking time for this dish is short and the baked prawns are succulent and juicy.

Fennel seeds 1 tsp, soaked for 10 minutes; drained before use

Cumin seeds 1 tsp, soaked for 10 minutes; drained before use

Vegetable oil as needed

Water 100 ml (3½ fl oz)

Coconut milk 100 ml (3½ fl oz)

Prawns (shrimps) 1 kg (2 lb 3 oz), large, peeled and deveined, leaving tails intact

Ground Paste

Candlenuts 6, sliced

Red chillies 6

Kaffir lime leaves 3

Ginger 5-cm (2-in) knob, peeled and chopped

Garlic 6 cloves, peeled

Onions 2, peeled and chopped

Dried prawn (shrimp) paste (*belacan*) 30 g (1 oz)

Salt to taste

1. Prepare ground paste. Combine all ingredients in a blender and process into a paste.
2. Combine fennel seeds and cumin seeds in a blender and process into a paste. Set aside.
3. Heat some oil in a wok over medium heat. Add ground paste and stir-fry until lightly browned and fragrant. Add water and stir in coconut milk. Bring to the boil, stirring continuously. When gravy begins to thicken and gets drier, remove from heat. Pour gravy into a large bowl.
4. Toss prawns into gravy and mix well. Then, rub fennel and cumin paste over prawns. Leave to stand for at least 30 minutes.
5. Preheat oven to 170°C (330°F). Arrange prawns in a baking dish and cover with aluminium foil. Bake for 15–20 minutes.
6. Serve hot with plain rice.

SAMBAL TUMIS UDANG

Serves 5–6

This chilli-based stew is one of the most popular and versatile Malay dishes and it has become indispensable as a heritage dish. *Sambal tumis udang* has an ideal blend of tastes—sourness from tamarind and spiciness from chilli. It can accompany a variety of dishes including *lontong sayur lodeh* (page 58), *nasi lemak* (page 50) and *nasi jagung* (page 64). Preparation requires a perfect combination of ingredients and of the best quality prawns. Our mother used to prepare this dish for festive occasions and home parties. One of my mother's godsons, Daud Yusof, would visit us just to eat this and nothing else! Till today, many of my friends still remember my mother and would often tell me how much they miss her cooking.

Vegetable oil as needed
Prawns (shrimps) 500 g (1 lb 1½ oz), tip of head, legs and feelers trimmed, deveined
Tamarind pulp 100 g (3½ oz), mixed with 250 ml (8 fl oz / 1 cup) water and strained
Salt to taste
Sugar 2 Tbsp or to taste
Water as needed

Ground Paste
Onions 3, peeled and chopped
Garlic 6 cloves, peeled
Dried chillies 15–20, soaked to soften, then cut into short lengths
Ginger 5-cm (2-in) knob, peeled
Dried prawn (shrimp) paste (*belacan*) 3-cm (1-in) square

1. Heat oil in a wok and add prawns. Stir-fry until prawns turn red and are cooked. Dish out and set aside.
2. Prepare ground paste. Combine all ingredients in a blender and process into a paste.
3. Reheat wok and add some oil. Add ground paste and stir-fry over medium heat until lightly browned and fragrant.
4. Stir in tamarind juice. Season with salt and sugar to taste.
5. Return prawns to wok and mix well. Add some water to adjust gravy to desired thickness and bring to the boil.
6. Dish out and serve hot with plain rice.

NOTE
- To make this dish less spicy, reduce the number of dried chillies used in the ground paste.

SAMBAL SOTONG DAGING SUMBAT

Serves 3–4

My mother used to modify traditional recipes to suit the tastes and preferences of family, friends and other guests. This dish is the result of one such recipe that my mother adapted from the traditional Malay dish, *sotong masak hitam* (squid in black sauce) as the colour of the dish did not appeal to my brother-in-law. Infused with various spices and with a thick sauce, this dish is best enjoyed with plain rice.

Squid 5, medium
Minced beef 250 g (9 oz)
Ground coriander 1 tsp
Ground cumin 1 tsp
Tapioca flour 1 Tbsp, mixed with some water into a paste
Vegetable oil as needed
Tamarind pulp 100 g (3 1/2 oz), mixed with 250 ml (8 fl oz / 1 cup) water and strained
Sugar to taste
Salt to taste
Ground white pepper 1 tsp

Ground Paste
Onions 2, peeled and sliced
Garlic 6 cloves, peeled
Candlenuts 3
Dried chillies 10, soaked to soften, then cut into short lengths
Red chillies 3
Dried prawn (shrimp) paste (*belacan*) 150 g (5 1/3 oz), chopped

1. Clean squid. Grip the tentacles in one hand and the squid tube in the other and pull them gently apart. The innards should slip out with the tentacles. Cut off the head and innards from the tentacles and discard. Squeeze out and remove the beak from the base of the tentacles. Rinse the tentacles and set aside. Remove and discard the thin sliver of cuttlebone from inside the squid tube. Peel off and discard the purplish outer skin from the squid tube. Rinse well.

2. Prepare ground paste. Combine all ingredients in a blender and process into a paste. Set aside.

3. In a shallow saucepan, dry-fry minced beef. When meat is nicely browned and cooked, add ground coriander and ground cumin. Mix well and cook until fragrant.

4. Stir in tapioca flour paste so meat binds together. Remove from heat and drain off excess liquid. Set meat aside to cool before stuffing into squid tubes. Seal stuffed squid tubes with the tentacles to keep stuffing in.

5. Heat some oil in a wok over medium heat. Add ground paste and stir-fry until fragrant and lightly browned.

6. Add tamarind juice, sugar, salt and pepper to taste. Bring to the boil.

7. Add stuffed squid and mix well. Leave to cook until squid are opaque and thoroughly cooked.

8. Dish out. Slice if desired and serve hot with plain rice.

MEAT & POULTRY

Bol Kentang Hajjah Zabidah 100

Rendang Daging 104

Rawon 106

Bergedil 108

Serunding Daging 110

Sambal Goreng 112

Kurma Ayam 114

Kari Ayam Melayu 116

Ayam Masak Merah 118

BOL KENTANG HAJJAH ZABIDAH

Serves 6–8

I have always been very intrigued by the mixture of tastes in this dish. We named this recipe after my mother as she made flavoursome modifications to the original recipe, making it her own and one of a kind. *Bol kentang Hajjah Zabidah* is essentially mashed potatoes stuffed with minced beef and rolled into a ball, then deep-fried, and served with a mildly sour soup that adds a pleasant contrast to the richness of the beef. In addition, the ground biscuits or breadcrumbs that wraps the ball gives a crispy texture that complements the fluidity of the soup. In our household, *bol kentang* is usually served during weekend family meals and small home parties. It is also an all-time favourite during Ramadhan. My mother would take down everyone's daily food requests for breaking our fast and this dish would usually top the list. Knowing how much my sisters and I loved this dish, my mother also used to prepare it to celebrate our birthdays.

Potatoes 2 kg (4 lb 6 oz), peeled and sliced in rounds
Vegetable oil as needed
Eggs 2, beaten, for coating
Breadcrumbs or crushed plain biscuits as needed, for coating
Crisp-fried shallots 2 Tbsp

Stuffing
Ginger 5-cm (2-in) knob, peeled
Garlic 10 cloves, peeled
Minced beef 500 g (1 lb 1½ oz)
Ground white pepper 2 tsp
Soup spices powder (*rempah sup*) 2 Tbsp
Onions 6, peeled and diced
Salt to taste

Tomato Soup
Dried chillies 5, soaked to soften, then cut into short lengths
Onions 3, peeled; 2 chopped and 1 sliced
Garlic 5 cloves, peeled
Cloves 3
Cardamoms 3
Star anise 2
Cinnamon 1 stick
Canned tomato soup 310 ml (10⅓ fl oz)
Soup spices powder (*rempah sup*) 2 Tbsp
Beef 300 g (11 oz), cut into cubes
Water 1 litre (32 fl oz / 4 cups)
Carrot 1, peeled and sliced
Tomato 1, cut into wedges
Salt to taste
Sugar to taste

1. Prepare tomato soup. Boil a small pot of water and add dried chillies. Boil for 3–5 minutes, then drain and set aside to cool. Combine boiled dried chillies, chopped onions and garlic in a blender and process into a paste. Set aside.
2. In a heavy saucepan, heat some oil over medium heat. Add sliced onion and stir-fry until lightly browned and fragrant.
3. Add cloves, cardamoms, star anise and cinnamon. Stir-fry until fragrant.
4. Add onion paste and stir-fry until well combined and fragrant.
5. Add tomato soup and soup spices powder. Mix well.
6. Add beef and cook for about 20 minutes until meat is tender. Add water and bring soup to the boil.
7. Add carrot and cook until tender. Add tomato and season with salt and sugar to taste. Bring to the boil, then remove from heat and set aside.
8. Prepare stuffing. Put ginger and garlic in a blender and process into a paste.
9. Heat some oil in a heavy saucepan over medium heat. Add ginger-garlic paste and stir-fry until lightly browned.
10. Add minced beef, stirring consistently until meat is cooked. Add pepper, soup spices powder and diced onions and stir-fry until well combined. Season with salt to taste and cook for a further 5 minutes before removing from heat. Drain excess liquid from stuffing. Set aside to cool.
11. Prepare potato croquettes. Heat enough oil for deep-frying and deep-fry sliced potatoes in batches until golden brown. Drain well.
12. Using a mortar and pestle, mash fried potato slices.
13. Form mashed potato into small balls, roughly 5–6 cm (2–2$^1/_2$ in) in diameter. Using your thumb, make a slight depression in each ball and fill with some stuffing. Fold the sides in to enclose stuffing completely. Repeat until ingredients are used up.
14. Dip balls in beaten egg, then coat with breadcrumbs or crushed biscuits. Pat crumbs firmly into balls.
15. Heat enough oil for deep-frying and deep-fry balls in batches until golden brown. Drain well.
16. To serve, place 2–3 potato croquettes in individual serving bowls or deep dishes. Ladle tomato soup over. Sprinkle with crisp-fried shallots and garnish as desired. Serve immediately.

RENDANG DAGING

Serves 4–6

There are generally two types of *rendang*—dry and wet. The meat is cooked in the gravy for several hours until the liquid evaporates, leaving the meat tender with the richness from the variety of spices used. Although beef is often used, it can be replaced with either chicken or mutton. *Rendang* is one of the most versatile dishes that I know of. It can accompany a variety of other dishes including *lontong sayur lodeh* (page 58), *roti kirai* (page 70) and *pulut kuning* (page 66). My mother's version is immersed in a thick gravy, making it good enough to be eaten on its own, with plain rice or even bread.

Vegetable oil as needed

Lemon grass 2 stalks, ends trimmed and slightly bruised

Galangal 5-cm (2-in) knob, peeled and slightly bruised

Kaffir lime leaves 5

Turmeric leaf 1

Beef 500 g (1 lb 1½ oz), cut into 4-cm (1½-in) lengths

Rendang **beef powder** 2 Tbsp

Water 300 ml (10 fl oz / 1¼ cups)

Coconut milk 200 ml (7 fl oz)

Salt to taste

Roasted coconut (*kerisik*) 3 Tbsp

Ground Paste

Dried chillies 10, soaked to soften, then cut into short lengths

Red chillies 4

Onions 2, peeled

Garlic 5 cloves, peeled

Ginger 5-cm (2-in) knob, peeled

Coriander seeds 1 Tbsp, soaked for 10 minutes; drained before use

Fennel seeds ½ tsp, soaked for 10 minutes; drained before use

Cumin seeds ½ tsp, soaked for 10 minutes; drained before use

1. Prepare ground paste. Combine all ingredients in a blender and process into a paste.
2. Heat some oil in a heavy saucepan over medium heat. Add ground paste and stir-fry until lightly browned and fragrant.
3. Add lemon grass, galangal, kaffir lime leaves and turmeric leaf one ingredient at a time. Bring to the boil.
4. Add *rendang* beef powder and mix well. Add water a little at a time, stirring well.
5. Add beef and cook over low heat for about an hour.
6. Add coconut milk a little at a time and mix well. Season with salt. Cook for another 45 minutes to an hour or until meat is tender. Leave gravy to boil until reduced to desired thickness.
7. Add roasted coconut and stir until well combined.
8. Dish out and serve with plain rice, *lontong sayur lodeh* (page 58) or *pulut kuning* (page 66).

RAWON

Serves 5–7

Buah keluak (Indonesian black nuts) adds a nutty flavour to the spices in this traditional stew. The nuts also give this dish its special dark colour. Often served with *bergedil* and its special *sambal belacan*, *rawon* is best eaten with plain rice. Even though my father prefers Indian cooking because of his roots, this Indonesian-influenced stew has such a distinctive, flavourful taste that it has become one of his personal favourites.

Beef including fatty meat 1 kg (2 lb 3 oz)
Water 3 litres (96 fl oz / 12 cups)
Vegetable oil as needed
Lemon grass 2 stalks, ends trimmed and bruised
Galangal 5-cm (2-in) knob, peeled and bruised
Kaffir lime leaves 7
Salt to taste
Sugar to taste
Crisp-fried shallots to taste

Spice Paste
Buah keluak (Indonesian black nuts) 7, soaked, then cracked to remove
Red chillies 2
Shallots 12, peeled
Garlic 7 cloves, peeled
Ginger 2.5-cm (1-in) knob, peeled
Turmeric 2.5-cm (1-in) knob, peeled
Coriander seeds 2 Tbsp
Fennel seeds 1 tsp, soaked for 10 minutes; drained before use
Cumin seeds 1 tsp, soaked for 10 minutes; drained before use
Candlenuts 4

1. Prepare *buah keluak* 3 days ahead. Wash, then soak nuts for 3 days, changing water daily. On day of cooking, crack cap of nuts using a pestle, remove the shell to make an opening, then remove kernel using a teaspoon. Set aside.
2. Prepare beef. Place beef and water in a heavy saucepan and cook over low heat for about an hour until meat is tender. To shorten cooking time, use a pressure cooker. Remove cooked beef and cut into small pieces, about 4–5-cm (1$^{1}/_{2}$–2-in). Return meat to stock and set aside.
3. Prepare spice paste. Put *buah keluak* kernels and all ingredients for spice paste in a blender and process into a paste.
4. Heat some oil in a frying pan over medium heat. Add spice paste and stir-fry until lightly browned and fragrant. Add some water while stir-frying if paste becomes too thick.
5. Add lemon grass, galangal and kaffir lime leaves and mix well.
6. Return spice paste to pan of boiled meat. Stir until well combined and bring to the boil. Season with salt and sugar to taste.
7. Dish out and garnish with crisp-fried shallots. Serve hot with plain rice and offer *sambal belacan* (page 31) and *bergedil* (page 108) on the side.

NOTE

- Ready-prepared *buah keluak* kernels can be purchased from some supermarkets. Simply soak the kernels in hot water for about 5 minutes and use as instructed in the recipe.

MEAT & POULTRY 107

BERGEDIL

Makes 20–25 pieces

Bergedil or potato cutlets are very much a part of Malay cuisine. My mother's *bergedil* is unique as she included minced beef in the mixture. The ones commonly found at restaurants and hawker centres are usually made using just mashed potatoes. *Bergedil* serves as a great accompaniment to rice and any side dish. It is also very moreish and you will not be able to stop at eating just one!

Vegetable oil for deep-frying
Potatoes 1 kg (2 lb 3 oz), peeled and sliced in rounds
Minced beef 250 g (9 oz)
Ground white pepper 1 Tbsp
Coriander leaves (cilantro) 10 g (1/3 oz), chopped
Spring onions (scallions) 10 g (1/3 oz), chopped
Crisp-fried shallots 3 Tbsp
Salt a pinch
Eggs 2, beaten

1. Heat oil for deep-frying and deep-fry sliced potatoes in batches until golden brown. Drain well.
2. Using a mortar and pestle, mash fried potato slices and set aside.
3. Heat some oil in a saucepan and add minced beef. Stir-fry lightly to cook. Drain excess oil and set aside.
4. In a large bowl, combine mashed potatoes, cooked minced beef, pepper, coriander leaves, spring onions and crisp-fried shallots. Season with a pinch of salt.
5. Form potato mixture into small balls.
6. Heat oil for deep-frying over medium-high heat.
7. Dip potato balls in beaten egg, then lower into hot oil. Cook in batches until golden brown. Drain well.

SERUNDING DAGING

Serves 5–10

Serunding daging is one of those foods I remember fondly from my childhood because it was cooked only during special occasions such as Eid. Coincidentally, it is also the favourite dish of my son, Syed Muhammad Luqman. Just like me, he likes to eat *serunding daging* on its own or sometimes with *lontong*. When I was studying at the University of Manchester in the UK and could not come home for Eid, my mother would send a package containing Hari Raya goodies and *serunding daging*. I would keep the *serunding daging* in the freezer and have it whenever I had a craving for it. *Serunding daging* will keep for up to a month when frozen.

Grated skinned coconut from 1 coconut

Vegetable oil 85 ml (2½ fl oz / ⅓ cup) or more as needed

Tamarind pulp 50 g (1⅔ oz), mixed with 400 ml (13⅓ fl oz) water and strained

Beef 500 g (1 lb 1½ oz), cut into 2.5-cm (1-in) cubes

Ground turmeric 1 Tbsp

Turmeric leaf 1

Kaffir lime leaves 7

Salt to taste

Palm sugar (*gula melaka*) 90 g (3¼ oz), grated

Spice Paste

Lemon grass 3 stalks, ends trimmed and cut into short lengths

Ginger 2.5-cm (1-in) knob, peeled and chopped

Galangal 2.5-cm (1-in) knob, peeled and chopped

Dried chillies 15, soaked to soften, then cut into short lengths

Onions 2, peeled and chopped

Garlic 5 cloves, peeled

Coriander seeds 2 Tbsp, soaked for 10 minutes; drained before use

Fennel seeds 1 tsp, soaked for 10 minutes; drained before use

Cumin seeds 1 tsp, soaked for 10 minutes; drained before use

1. Heat a large wok over low heat. Add grated coconut and dry-fry until lightly browned. Dish out and set aside.
2. Prepare spice paste. Combine all ingredients in a blender and process into a paste.
3. Heat oil in a clean wok over medium heat. Add spice paste and stir-fry until lightly browned and fragrant. Add tamarind juice and meat. Stir-fry until meat is cooked.
4. Add ground turmeric, turmeric leaf and kaffir lime leaves. Season with salt and palm sugar. Leave to cook until meat is tender.
5. Add dry-fried grated coconut and stir continuously until well combined.
6. For special occasions such as Eid, serve *serunding daging* with *lontong sayur lodeh* (page 58), *rendang daging* (page 104) and *sambal goreng* (page 112). On normal occasions, serve it as an accompaniment to plain rice.

SAMBAL GORENG

Serves 5–8

The preparation of this dish may appear cumbersome but once you taste it, you will appreciate the effort put into making it. This side dish is often served with a staple such as *lontong* or plain rice. Although its name may imply that the dish is spicy, it is in fact mild with a rather sweet taste. My mother and her eldest sister, Hajjah Raftah, learnt how to prepare *sambal goreng* from their mother. Both ladies were keen helpers in their mother's kitchen. My sisters and I learned from early in our youth that observing and being involved in the kitchen are the best ways to inherit traditional recipes. Until today, my mother's *sambal goreng* is a dish our guests look forward to when they visit during Eid.

Beef 250 g (9 oz)

Beef liver 200 g (7 oz)

Beef lung 200 g (7 oz)

Vegetable oil as needed

Prawns (shrimps) 500 g (1 lb 1$^1/_2$ oz) medium, peeled and deveined

Tempeh 2 pieces, diced

Firm bean curd 4 pieces, diced

Dried chillies 3, soaked to soften, then cut into short lengths

Onion 1, peeled and finely sliced

Garlic 3, peeled and finely sliced

Lemon grass 2 stalks, ends trimmed and finely sliced

Galangal 2.5-cm (1-in) knob, peeled and sliced

Ginger 2.5-cm (1-in) knob, peeled and sliced

Green chillies 2, sliced

Palm sugar (*gula melaka*) 200 g (7 oz)

Coconut milk 350 ml (11$^2/_3$ fl oz)

Salt to taste

Crisp-fried shallots 300 g (11 oz)

Ground Paste

Dried chillies 15, soaked to soften, then cut into short lengths

Onions 2, peeled and chopped

Garlic 5 cloves, peeled

Dried prawn (shrimp) paste (*belacan*) 50 g (1$^2/_3$ oz)

1. Boil beef, beef liver and beef lung in a heavy saucepan for about 45 minutes or until meat is tender. To shorten cooking time, use a pressure cooker. Remove cooked meat and cut into cubes. Set aside.
2. Heat enough oil for deep-frying and deep-fry cooked beef, beef liver, beef lung, prawns, tempeh and firm bean curd separately. Drain well and set aside.
3. With just a little oil, stir-fry dried chillies, onion, garlic, lemon grass, galangal, ginger and green chillies separately. Drain well and set aside.
4. Prepare ground paste. Put all ingredients in a blender and process into a paste.
5. Heat some oil in a large wok. Add ground paste and stir-fry until lightly browned and fragrant. Add palm sugar and coconut milk. Bring to the boil, stirring continuously.
6. Add all deep-fried and stir-fried ingredients and mix well. Season with salt to taste. Stir in crisp-fried shallots, then dish out onto a serving plate.
7. For special occasions such as Eid, serve with *lontong sayur lodeh* (page 58) and *rendang daging* (page 104). On normal occasions, serve as an accompaniment to plain rice.

KURMA AYAM

Serves 6–8

Kurma ayam or chicken korma is an Indian-influenced curry dish which is non-spicy and light-coloured. With the use of a korma powder, this curry tastes different from other curries and its mild flavours make it suitable even for children. It can be paired beautifully with any rice dish, plain bread or naan but it is best served with *nasi jagung* (page 64). It is also a versatile dish and chicken can be substituted with beef or mutton.

Vegetable oil as needed

Onion 1, peeled and sliced

Cloves 2

Cardamoms 2

Korma spice powder 2 Tbsp

Water 1 litre (32 fl oz / 4 cups)

Coconut milk 400 ml (13$\frac{1}{3}$ fl oz)

Chicken 1, medium, cut into 8–12 pieces

Potatoes 2, peeled and cut to quarters

Almonds 10, soaked, skinned and coarsely ground

Green chillies 2, slit midway

Salt to taste

Tomato 1, cut into quarters

Crisp-fried shallots 2 Tbsp

Ground Paste

Onions 2, peeled and chopped

Garlic 7 cloves, peeled

Ginger 5-cm (2-in) knob, peeled

Red chillies 2

Green chillies 2

1. Prepare ground paste. Put all ingredients in a blender and process into a paste.
2. Heat some oil in a heavy saucepan over medium heat. Add sliced onion and stir-fry until lightly browned and fragrant.
3. Add ground paste and stir-fry until fragrant.
4. Add cloves, cardamoms and korma spice powder and stir-fry until well combined.
5. Add water, coconut milk and chicken. Cook for about 10 minutes, then add potatoes. Mix well and let gravy simmer until chicken is cooked and potatoes are tender.
6. Add coarsely ground almonds, then green chillies. Season with salt to taste.
7. Bring to the boil, then add tomato and crisp-fried shallots.
8. Dish out and serve hot with plain rice.

KARI AYAM MELAYU

Serves 6–8

My paternal grandfather, Alal Mohamed Russull, came from Sri Lanka. He was a businessman who played a major role in financing the first Malay women's welfare home headed by my grandmother. He also shared her vision of giving back to the community and welcomed any suggestions to empower the Malays especially in the spirit of entrepreneurship. Sri Lanka is renowned for its exotic spices and my grandfather brought his native cuisine and spices to Singapore, resulting in a rich diversity of cooking styles and techniques in the family kitchen. Spices also found its way into my mother's cooking to cater to my father's taste. As a result, my mother created a few dishes that are a fusion of Indian and Malay cuisine. She presented traditional Indian curry with a fresh and vibrant Malay twist, as such with this chicken curry.

Vegetable oil as needed
Onion 1, peeled and sliced
Cloves 3
Cardamoms 3
Star anise 3
Cinnamon 1 stick
Curry leaves 5 stalks
Beef curry powder 2 Tbsp
Water 1 litre (32 fl oz / 4 cups)
Chicken 1, medium, cut into 8–12 pieces
Potatoes 2, peeled and cut into quarters
Coconut milk 400 ml (13$^1/_3$ fl oz)
Green and red chillies 2 each, slit midway

Tomato 1, cut into quarters
Salt to taste
Sugar to taste
Crisp-fried shallots 2 Tbsp

Ground Paste
Dried chillies 5–7, soaked to soften, then cut into short lengths
Onions 2, peeled and chopped
Garlic 7 cloves, peeled
Ginger 5-cm (2-in) knob, peeled and chopped
Green chillies 3

1. Prepare ground paste. Put all ingredients in a blender and process into a paste.
2. Heat some oil in a heavy saucepan over medium heat. Add sliced onion and stir-fry until lightly browned. Add cloves, cardamoms, star anise and cinnamon and stir-fry until fragrant. Toss in curry leaves.
3. Add ground paste and stir-fry for a few minutes. Add curry powder and mix well.
4. When the mixture is well combined, add some of the water, stir the ingredients, then add chicken. Cook for about 10 minutes, then add potatoes and the remaining water. Mix well and let gravy simmer until chicken is cooked and potatoes are tender.
5. Stir in coconut milk and add chillies. Bring to the boil.
6. Add tomato and season with salt and sugar to taste. Add crisp-fried shallots.
7. Dish out and serve hot with plain rice.

AYAM MASAK MERAH

Serves 6–8

Ayam masak merah or chicken in chilli and tomato sauce is a popular Malay dish that is often served with plain rice, *nasi minyak* or *nasi jagung* (page 64) on celebratory occasions. It is most commonly served at Malay weddings but is also frequently prepared as a household favourite. *Ayam masak merah* has an interesting spicy yet sweet taste—a result of the combination of spices and the tomato-based paste. This combination also produces an alluring aroma, which is what makes this dish so inviting.

Chicken 1, medium, cut into 8–12 pieces
Ground turmeric 1 tsp
Salt a pinch
Vegetable oil for deep-frying
Onion 1, peeled and thinly sliced
Garlic 3 cloves, peeled and chopped
Ginger 2.5-cm (1-in) knob, peeled and thinly sliced
Galangal 5-cm (2-in) knob, peeled and thinly sliced
Lemon grass 3 stalks, ends trimmed and thinly sliced

Curry leaves 3 stalks
Tomato purée 2 Tbsp
Coconut milk 100 ml (3½ fl oz)
Salt to taste
Sugar to taste
Crisp-fried shallots 2 Tbsp

Ground Paste

Dried chillies 15–20, soaked to soften, then cut into short lengths
Onions 2, peeled and chopped
Garlic 6 cloves, peeled

1. Marinate chicken with ground turmeric and salt. Leave to stand for about 15 minutes.
2. Heat oil for deep-frying and deep-fry chicken for 5–7 minutes or until chicken is half-cooked. Drain and set aside.
3. Prepare ground paste. Put all ingredients into a blender and process into a paste.
4. Heat some oil in a heavy saucepan over medium heat. Add sliced onion and chopped garlic and stir-fry until lightly browned and fragrant.
5. Add ginger, galangal and lemon grass and mix well.
6. Add curry leaves and continue to stir-fry until fragrant.
7. Add ground paste to pan, stirring continuously until fragrant. Add tomato purée and mix well.
8. Add half-cooked chicken, then coconut milk. Season with salt and sugar to taste. Leave to boil until chicken is cooked.
9. Add crisp-fried shallots and dish out. Serve hot with plain rice.

VEGETABLES

Sambal Jengganan Che Zahara Kaum Ibu 122

Semur Daging 124

Kangkong Belacan 126

Chap Chye 128

Mahshi Kobis Hubaba 130

Acar Timun 132

Paceri Nenas 134

SAMBAL JENGGANAN CHE ZAHARA KAUM IBU

Serves 6–8

Sambal jengganan brings back special memories for my family. This particular version is named after my late grandmother, Che Zahara. My auntie, Hajjah Fatimah, recalls how both she and my grandmother would prepare free meals for the needy. They served *sambal jengganan* in large platters (see photograph on page 13). My father recalls joining the orphans in the communal meals as my grandmother believed that "the best food is food shared by many and blessings reside in those who eat together." Although my sisters and I were not yet born at the peak of our grandmother's community work, her contributions in the past have a continual impact on the present. She is still remembered for her unmatched kindness and selfless generosity today. In recognition of her contribution to Singapore's heritage, the National Heritage Board has placed her among other prominent personalities including Ahmad Ibrahim (former Member of Parliament during Singapore's founding years) at the Bidadari Memorial Park, Choa Chu Kang Cemetery. She is also featured in the museum at the Malay Heritage Centre.

Vegetable oil as needed
Firm bean curd 3, pieces
Tempeh 2 pieces
Bean sprouts 150 g (5$^1/_3$ oz)
Long beans 100 g (3$^1/_2$ oz), cut into 4-cm (1$^1/_2$-in) lengths
Green cabbage 150 g (5$^1/_3$ oz), thinly sliced
Hard-boiled eggs 2, peeled and cut into wedges

Spicy Peanut Sauce
Raw skinned peanuts 200 g (7 oz)
Dried chillies 20, soaked to soften, then cut into short lengths
Garlic 3 cloves, peeled and thinly sliced
Dried prawn (shrimp) paste (*belacan*) 150 g (5$^1/_3$ oz)
Tamarind pulp 150 g (5$^1/_3$ oz), mixed with 250 ml (8 fl oz / 1 cup) water and strained
Salt to taste
Sugar 2 Tbsp

1. Prepare spicy peanut sauce. Heat some oil in a pan and fry peanuts until lightly browned. Remove and drain. Repeat to fry dried chillies, garlic and dried prawn paste separately for 30 seconds each. Set aside and allow to cool.
2. Using a mortar and pestle, grind peanuts coarsely. Repeat to grind dried chillies, garlic and dried prawn paste together into a paste. Alternatively, use a blender.
3. Pour paste into a heavy saucepan. Add tamarind juice and bring to the boil over medium heat for a few minutes. Add ground peanuts. Season with salt and sugar to taste. Adjust consistency of sauce with some water if desired.
4. Prepare other ingredients. Heat enough oil for deep-frying and deep-fry bean curd and tempeh. Drain well and slice.
5. Boil a pot of water and add a pinch of salt. Blanch bean sprouts, long beans and cabbage separately. Drain well.
6. Arrange ingredients in a large serving dish with a bowl of spicy peanut sauce. Serve hot on its own or with plain rice.

VEGETABLES 123

SEMUR DAGING

Serves 5–6

There is a wide range of ingredients used in different recipes for *semur daging* or beef stew. However, this family recipe calls for nothing more than chunks of beef and slices of crispy fried bean curd. It is a simple but filling meal that is ideal for cold weather or rainy days.

Vegetable oil as needed
Firm bean curd 5 pieces, each cut into 4 triangles
Beef 500 g (1 lb 1½ oz), cut into large pieces
Water 1 litre (32 fl oz / 4 cups)
Red chillies 2, thinly sliced
Galangal 5-cm (2-in) knob, peeled
Ground nutmeg ½ tsp
Ground white pepper 2 tsp
Spring onions (scallions) 5, finely chopped

Sweet soy sauce 5 tsp
Salt to taste
Sugar to taste
Tomato 1, cut into wedges
Crisp-fried shallots 2 Tbsp

Ground Paste
Onions 2, peeled and chopped
Garlic 6 cloves, peeled

1. Heat enough oil for deep-frying and deep-fry bean curd triangles until lightly browned. Drain and set aside.
2. Place beef and water in a heavy saucepan and cook over low heat until meat is well done. Remove beef, cut into pieces and return to pan. Leave to simmer.
3. Prepare ground paste. Put onion and garlic in a blender and process into a paste. Add paste to pan.
4. Add fried bean curd to pan and continue to simmer over low heat.
5. Heat oil in a frying pan over low heat. Add chillies, galangal, ground nutmeg, pepper and spring onions. Stir-fry until lightly browned and fragrant.
6. Add contents of frying pan to saucepan of beef. Add sweet soy sauce and season with salt and sugar to taste.
7. Add tomato and bring to the boil.
8. Dish out and garnish with crisp-fried shallots. Serve hot with plain rice.

KANGKONG BELACAN

Serves 5–6

Dishes such as *nasi lemak* are never complete without *kangkong belacan* as a side dish. This dish of stir-fried water spinach with dried prawn (shrimp) paste (*belacan*) is also a popular accompaniment to seafood dishes such as *ikan bakar*. The dried prawn (shrimp) paste in this dish gives it a distinctly Malay taste, yet the pungency that comes with this paste is drowned by aromas from the other ingredients. The combination of chilli and garlic gives a rich taste that complements the mild flavour of water spinach itself.

Vegetable oil as needed
Onion 1, peeled and thinly sliced
Garlic 3 cloves, peeled and chopped
Red and green chillies 1 each, thinly sliced
Kangkong **(water spinach)** 1 bundle
Belacan **stock granules** 1 tsp
Salt to taste
Sugar to taste

1. Heat oil in a saucepan over medium heat. Add onion and garlic and stir-fry until lightly browned.
2. Add chillies, then spinach and *belacan* stock granules. Mix well.
3. Season with salt and sugar to taste.
4. Dish out and serve immediately.

NOTE
- Do not overcook *kangkong*. This is to ensure that its nutrients are retained.
- Dried prawn (shrimp) paste (*belacan*) can be used in place of *belacan* stock granules. Just fry in a pan without any oil until paste is dry and crumbly.

CHAP CHYE

Serves 5–6

This recipe is Chinese-inspired. *Chap chye* is a stir-fried mixed vegetable dish of button mushrooms, cauliflower, broccoli, baby corn, pea pods, green and red capsicums (bell peppers). My mother would also include ingredients such as squid and prawns (shrimps), producing a dish that is quite different from other stir-fried vegetable dishes. Use the freshest ingredients you can find. Cooking this dish is actually very easy.

Vegetable oil as needed
Garlic 7 cloves, peeled and bruised
Beef 100 g (3½ oz), cut into small pieces
Squid 1, cleaned and thinly sliced
Prawns (shrimps) 5, peeled and deveined, leaving tails intact
Button mushrooms 50 g (1⅔ oz), halved
Fishcake 1, sliced
Sesame oil 2 tsp
Oyster sauce 3 Tbsp
Ground white pepper 1 tsp
Cauliflower 100 g (3½ oz), cut into florets
Broccoli 100 g (3½ oz)
Baby corn 100 g (3½ oz)
Snow peas 100 g (3½ oz)
Carrot 1, peeled and sliced
Red and green capsicums (bell peppers) 1, cored and seeded, sliced
Onions 2, large, peeled and cut into quarters
Corn flour 2 Tbsp
Water 300 ml (10 fl oz / 1¼ cups)
Salt to taste
Sugar to taste

1. Heat some oil in a wok over medium heat. Add garlic and stir-fry until lightly browned and fragrant.
2. Add beef, squid and prawns. Stir-fry for a few minutes.
3. Add button mushrooms and fishcake. Season with sesame oil, oyster sauce and pepper. Mix well.
4. Add cauliflower, broccoli, baby corn, snow peas, carrot, capsicums and onions. Stir-fry to mix.
5. Mix corn flour with water and add to wok. Bring to a simmer, then season with salt and sugar to taste. Stir-fry for a few minutes, then remove from heat.
6. Dish out and serve hot with plain rice or *nasi ayam* (page 54).

NOTE

- For instructions to clean squid, refer to page 96.

MAHSHI KOBIS HUBABA

Serves 6–8

This dish of minced beef wrapped in cabbage leaves is originally an Arabic dish. I learned this recipe from my mother-in-law. It deviates from the conventional vegetable stew in Malay cuisine because the vegetables are not added to the soup. Instead, the beef filling is wrapped in crunchy cabbage leaves, creating a contrasting texture and providing flavour with every bite. Served in a tomato-based sauce, *mahshi kobis Hubaba* is a refreshing and versatile dish that can be served for lunch or dinner.

Green cabbage leaves as needed
Garlic 5 cloves, peeled
Vegetable oil as needed
Minced beef 500 g (1 lb 1½ oz)
Ground white pepper 1 tsp
Soup spices powder (*rempah sup*) 2 Tbsp
Onions 3, peeled and cut into cubes
Salt to taste
Sugar to taste
Coriander leaves (cilantro) 3 sprigs, finely chopped
Crisp-fried shallots (optional) 2 Tbsp

Sauce
Onion 1, peeled
Garlic 3, peeled
Ground white pepper 1 tsp
Soup spices powder (*rempah sup*) 1 tsp
Tomato purée 2 Tbsp
Water 300 ml (10 fl oz / 1¼ cups), or as needed to obtain desired thickness of gravy
Salt to taste
Sugar to taste
Tomato 1, cut into quarters
Coriander leaves (cilantro) 3 sprigs

1. In a steamer, steam cabbage leaves for about 10 minutes. When leaves have softened, separate them.
2. Put garlic in a blender and process into a paste. Heat some oil in a large saucepan over high heat. Add garlic paste and stir-fry until lightly browned and fragrant.
3. Add minced beef and stir-fry, breaking up any lumps that form. Cook until meat is lightly browned. Season with pepper and soup spices powder. Mix well.
4. Add onions and continue to stir-fry for a few minutes. Season with salt and sugar to taste. Add coriander leaves and crisp-fried shallots. Stir-fry to mix well. Dish out.
5. Place a cabbage leaf, inside up, on a chopping board. Spoon some beef mixture onto leaf. Fold sides of leaf in over filling, then roll leaf firmly to enclose filling. Repeat to make more rolls until beef mixture is used up. Set rolls aside.
6. Prepare sauce. Put onion and garlic in a blender and process into a paste. Heat some oil in a heavy saucepan. Add onion and garlic paste and stir-fry until lightly browned and fragrant. Add pepper and soup spices powder and mix well.
7. Stir in tomato purée. Add water so paste is not too thick. Mix well for about 5 minutes and bring to the boil. Season with salt and sugar to taste. Add tomato and coriander leaves.
8. To serve, arrange cabbage rolls, seam side down, on a serving dish. Pour sauce over. Garnish as desired and serve hot with plain rice.

NOTE

- To help the cabbage leaves roll up more easily, cut a deep V from the stem end of the leaf before steaming. This removes the thickest part of the centre rib of the leaves.

ACAR TIMUN

Serves 6–10

Acar timun is a cucumber and carrot pickle and is incredibly easy to make. It is a great accompaniment to most rice dishes such as briyani rice or *kurma ayam* (page 114). You can also enjoy this pickle on its own. Savour the sweet and sour flavours as they dance on your taste buds.

Vegetable oil as needed

Shallots 5, peeled and left whole

Red and green chillies 2 each, halved and soaked in salted water

Ground turmeric 1/2 Tbsp

Vinegar 1 Tbsp

Salt to taste

Sugar 1 Tbsp

Cucumber 1, halved, soft centre removed and cut into 3-cm (1-in) lengths

Carrot 1, peeled and cut into 3-cm (1-in) lengths

Ground Paste

Dried chillies 7–10, soaked to soften, then cut into short lengths

Garlic 6 cloves, peeled

Ginger 5-cm (2-in) knob, peeled and chopped

1. Prepare ground paste. Place dried chillies, garlic and ginger in a blender and process into a paste.
2. Heat some oil in a wok over low heat. Add ground paste and stir-fry until lightly browned and fragrant.
3. Add shallots and chillies, stirring constantly.
4. Add ground turmeric and vinegar and season with salt and sugar to taste.
5. Add sliced cucumber and carrot. Bring to the boil.
6. Dish out and leave to cool before serving as an accompaniment to plain rice or special briyani rice.

NOTE

- Adjust the spiciness of this dish by varying the number of dried chillies used in the ground paste.

PACERI NENAS

Serves 5–6

Paceri nenas is a popular fruit-based recipe served during traditional Malay weddings, festive occasions and formal luncheons and dinners. Spices like cloves, cardamoms and star anise add flavour to the sweet natural taste of ripe pineapple.

Vegetable oil as needed
Garlic 3 cloves, peeled and sliced
Onion 1, peeled and sliced
Cloves 3
Cardamoms 3
Star anise 3
Cinnamon 1 stick
Red and green chillies 1 each, slit midway
Water 1 litre (32 fl oz / 4 cups)
Yellow food colouring 1 tsp
Ripe pineapple 1, medium, about 600 g (1 lb 5$^1/_3$ oz), peeled, cored and cut into small pieces
Salt to taste
Sugar to taste

1. Heat some oil in a saucepan over medium heat. Add garlic and onion and stir-fry until lightly browned and fragrant.
2. Add cloves, cardamoms, star anise, cinnamon and chillies. Stir-fry for about 5 minutes or until lightly browned, then add water and bring to the boil.
3. Stir in colouring and add pineapple. Cook for about 10 minutes.
4. Season with salt and sugar to taste. Remove from heat.
5. Dish out and leave to cool before serving as an accompaniment to plain rice or special briyani rice.

COOKIES & CAKES

Biskut Kacang Madu Cornflakes 138
Kuih Tart Klasik 140
Biskut Suji 142
Kuih Makmur 144
Biskut Coklat Putih Pistachio 146
Biskut Coklat Chip Kayu Manis 148
Kek Kukus 150
Kek Marmar 152
Kek Potong Biskut Coklat dan Kismis 154
Kek Brownie Tiga-Coklat Kacang Walnut 156

BISKUT KACANG MADU CORNFLAKES

Makes about 100 pieces

As an ingredient, cornflakes have been used in every way imaginable, in appetisers, desserts, snacks and cookies. During festive seasons, a popular cookie recipe using cornflakes is honey cornflakes. I first had a taste of these at a friend's house when I was about 15 years old. I remember I loved them so much that I ate five at a go. It's one of those cookies that once you start eating, you just can't stop. Thus, began my quest to make my own. I must have tried at least five different recipes growing up and my mother was always patient, indulging me in my baking adventures. This particular cookie was one of the reasons I started baking and continue to love the process, even today.

Almonds 60 g ($2^{1}/_{4}$ oz)
Cashew nuts 60 g ($2^{1}/_{4}$ oz)
Unsalted butter 125 g ($4^{1}/_{2}$ oz)
Honey 4 Tbsp
Castor sugar 2 Tbsp
Premium quality cornflakes 130 g ($4^{2}/_{3}$ oz)
Mini cupcake paper cases about 100

1. Preheat oven to 150°C (300°F).
2. Place almonds and cashew nuts on a baking tray and toast lightly in the oven for about 5 minutes. Leave to cool before chopping.
3. In a large saucepan, melt butter over medium heat. When butter is beginning to boil, add honey and 1 Tbsp sugar. Stir constantly for a few minutes until mixture is simmering.
4. Remove from heat and add cornflakes, almonds and cashew nuts, stirring quickly. Sprinkle remaining 1 Tbsp sugar over and mix well.
5. Using a teaspoon, scoop mixture into paper cases. Place onto baking trays and bake for 12–15 minutes.
6. Leave to cool completely before storing in airtight containers.

NOTE

- Vary the nuts used as desired or omit completely for those allergic to peanuts.

COOKIES & CAKES 139

KUIH TART KLASIK

Makes about 100 tarts

In Singapore, festive celebrations, from Chinese New Year to Eid are incomplete without the pineapple tart or *kuih tart klasik*. This festive cookie can be found in almost every household during the festive season. It is also one of my mother's personal favourites. Her recipe produces a rich, buttery, melt-in-your-mouth pastry. In our family, it is common practice to exchange goodies during Eid and my mother's pineapple tarts are among the top two most-loved treats. She would give away 50 to 100 of these tarts to each of our close relatives and friends every year. Pineapple tarts are so popular in Singapore that they are now easily available all year round at bakeries.

Pastry

Baking powder 1/8 tsp

Plain (all-purpose) flour 500 g (1 lb 1 1/2 oz), sifted

Unsalted butter 250 g (9 oz), at room temperature

Sweetened condensed milk 2 1/2 Tbsp

Ghee 2 Tbsp

Fine salt 1/4 tsp

Egg yolks from 2 eggs

Egg white from 1 egg

Vanillin powder 1/4 tsp

Pineapple Jam

Unripe pineapples 5, peeled, cut into small pieces and strained

Pandan leaves 2, tied into a knot

Castor sugar 250 g (9 oz)

Lemon juice 1/8 tsp

Vanilla essence 1/8 tsp

1. Prepare pineapple jam. Place pineapple pieces in a saucepan with pandan leaves, stirring continuously over medium heat until mixture thickens. Add sugar, lemon juice and vanilla essence and continue stirring until mixture takes on a jam-like texture. Continue to stir for about 10 minutes or until filling is dry. Leave to cool completely.

2. Prepare pastry. Sift together baking powder and flour. Set aside.

3. Using an electric mixer, cream butter until light and smooth. Add condensed milk, ghee and salt. Beat until well combined. Add eggs and vanillin powder. Beat for 3 minutes.

4. Add sifted flour gradually in batches until well combined. Knead pastry until firm and of an even consistency. Leave to rest for 10 minutes.

5. With a rolling pin, roll pastry out to a thickness of about 0.5-cm (1/4-in). Cut pastry into rounds using a tart mould and clip edges with a cookie pincher for that home-made look. Arrange on a baking tray.

6. Roll cooled pineapple jam into small balls about 2.5-cm (1-in) in diameter. Flatten them slightly, then place in the centre of shaped pastry. Repeat until ingredients are used up.

7. Preheat oven to 160°C (325°F). Bake tarts for 20–25 minutes or until pastry is lightly browned.

NOTE

- The pineapple jam can be made in advance and kept refrigerated. Many local baking shops and supermarkets also stock ready-made pineapple jam. A 1 kg (2 lb 3 oz) pack would be more than sufficient for this recipe.

COOKIES & CAKES 141

BISKUT SUJI

Makes 100–120 cookies

Biskut suji is popularly prepared in many Malay households during Eid. I particularly love making this cookie because it is one of my father's favourite cookies. When I bake and serve them hot from the oven, my father's eyes will simply sparkle. My mother's home-made version of this cookie is really simple to do and tends to be bite-sized compared to those found at bakeries. These cookies provide another melt-in-your-mouth moment.

Ghee 250 g (9 oz)
Icing (confectioner's) sugar 250 g (9 oz), sifted
Fine salt 1/4 tsp
Vanilla essence 1/2 tsp
Plain (all-purpose) flour 520 g (1 lb 2 1/2 oz), sifted

1. Preheat oven to 160°C (325°F).
2. Beat ghee until softened, then add icing sugar, salt and vanilla essence. When mixture is well combined, add flour a little at a time until well incorporated.
3. Using a 1-tsp measure, scoop up 1 tsp dough and roll into a ball. Place on a baking tray. Repeat until dough is used up.
4. Bake cookies for 20–25 minutes or until lightly browned.
5. Leave cookies to cool completely on a wire rack before storing in airtight containers.

NOTE

- As there tends to be lumps in icing sugar, sifting it before use will help to prevent lumps in the dough.
- Using a measuring spoon to scoop up the dough for rolling helps keep the cookies uniform in shape and size. A 1-tsp measure yields 100–120 medium-size cookies and a 1-Tbsp measure will yield 40–60 large cookies.

KUIH MAKMUR

Makes 50–60 cookies

This traditional recipe was modified by my mother. She added ghee as an ingredient to make the dough softer. The resulting cookie has a texture similar to that of her *kuih tart klasik* (page 140). *Kuih makmur* or prosperity cookie requires lots of patience to make as well as nimble and meticulous hands, as the pattern on the dough is clipped best by hand and not with a cookie mould. I have a penchant for making cookies (even if it takes hours) and I hope you do too! It is also with this meticulous attitude that I recorded my mother's kitchen secrets as I helped her in the kitchen. *Kuih makmur* is another household favourite that has been part of our family gatherings on many occasions.

Unsalted butter 160 g (5 $^{3}/_{4}$ oz), at room temperature
Ghee 100 g (3 $^{1}/_{2}$ oz)
Fine salt $^{1}/_{4}$ tsp
Castor sugar 110 g (4 oz)
Egg 1
Vanillin powder $^{1}/_{2}$ tsp
Plain (all-purpose) flour 320 g (11$^{1}/_{2}$ oz), sifted
Icing (confectioner's) sugar as needed

Filling
Cashew nuts 80 g (2$^{4}/_{5}$ oz)
Castor sugar 1 tsp
Butter 20 g ($^{2}/_{3}$ oz), melted

1. Prepare filling. Heat a pan over medium heat and dry-fry cashew nuts for a few minutes until lightly browned. Remove from heat and leave to cool. Crush cooled nuts coarsely using a food chopper. Mix nuts with sugar and melted butter. Stir until well combined. Set aside.
2. Using an electric mixer, beat butter, ghee, salt and sugar until creamy and smooth.
3. Add egg and vanillin powder and stir well. Continue to stir mixture while adding flour a little at a time until dough is formed.
4. To make cookies, pinch a bit of dough and roll into an oval shape. Press it in your palm to create a well in the middle. It should resemble a leaf.
5. Spoon some filling into the well, then bring sides of dough up to enclose filling. Clip dough using a cookie pincher to create veins of leaf. Place on an ungreased baking tray.
6. Repeat steps to make cookies until ingredients are used up.
7. Preheat oven to 170°C (330°F). Bake cookies for 25–30 minutes or until lightly browned.
8. Leave cookies to cool completely before dusting lightly with icing sugar. Store in an airtight container until ready to serve.

NOTE

- Vary the filling by using peanuts instead of cashew nuts.
- To keep the size of the cookies consistent, use a measuring spoon to portion out the dough. Alternatively, use a digital weighing scale.

COOKIES & CAKES 145

BISKUT COKLAT PUTIH PISTACHIO

Makes about 90 cookies

Chocolate is a modern ingredient but my mother was always open to new ideas and recipes. When we first saw this recipe, she wanted to try it immediately. Her instincts were right. The cookies turned out great. After she added her personal touch and made some modifications, this recipe quickly become part of our annual staple during Eid. This biscuit is deliciously topped with white chocolate and toasted pistachios. The dough also has a unique texture and taste as it contains coarsely-crushed rolled oats.

Pistachio nuts 200 g (7 oz)
Unsalted butter 200 g (7 oz), at room temperature
Castor sugar 100 g ($3^{1}/_{2}$ oz)
Emplex $^{1}/_{2}$ tsp
Vanillin powder 1 tsp
Salt $^{1}/_{4}$ tsp
Rolled oats 80 g ($2^{4}/_{5}$ oz), coarsely crushed
Rice flour 40 g ($1^{1}/_{3}$ oz)
Top flour 200 g (7 oz), sifted
White chocolate 250 g (9 oz), chopped

1. Preheat oven to 160°C (325°F).
2. Place pistachio nuts on a baking tray and toast lightly in the oven for about 5 minutes. Leave to cool before chopping. Set aside. Keep oven heated.
3. Using an electric mixer, cream butter, sugar, emplex, vanillin powder and salt together until light and fluffy. Add rolled oats, rice flour and top flour a little at a time until well combined.
4. With a rolling pin, roll dough out to a thickness of about 0.5-cm ($^{1}/_{4}$-in). Using cookie cutters, cut out cookies and place them on unlined baking trays.
5. Bake cookies for 12–15 minutes or until lightly browned. Leave to cool on a wire rack.
6. Place chocolate in a double boiler or a bowl placed over a pot of boiling water. Stir until chocolate is melted and smooth.
7. Brush top of cookies with melted chocolate, then drop chopped pistachios on chocolate while still wet. Leave chocolate to set before storing cookies in airtight containers.

NOTE

- Emplex is an emulsifier that is added to bread and pastry doughs to give baked products a soft and springy texture.
- Top flour is an extra-fine quality flour that gives cakes and cookies a fine and smooth texture. If unavailable, plain (all-purpose) flour can be used as a substitute.

COOKIES & CAKES 147

BISKUT COKLAT CHIP KAYU MANIS

Makes about 100 small cookies

Chocolate chip cookies are an American creation, but my family has adopted the recipe and included ingredients such as cinnamon or ground nutmeg into the dough for additional flavour and texture. This chocolate chip cinnamon cookie is a hit among my children and nephews. Made with unsalted butter and a combination of premium chocolate morsels, it produces a rich and chewy cookie with caramelised edges. This recipe is also versatile. For example, coffee lovers can substitute chocolate emulco with coffee oil, and the nuts can be replaced as desired.

Egg 1
Vanilla essence 1 tsp
Chocolate emulco 1/2 tsp
Hazelnuts 70 g (2 1/2 oz)
Almonds 70 g (2 1/2 oz)
Unsalted butter 250 g (9 oz), at room temperature
Light brown sugar 200 g (7 oz)

Salt 1/4 tsp
Ground cinnamon (optional) 1/2 tsp or 1 tsp for a stronger flavour
Oats or Nestum mixed cereal 1/4 cup
Ground almonds 1/4 cup
Premium semi-sweet chocolate morsels/chunks 200 g (7 oz)
Plain (all-purpose) flour 500 g (1 lb 1 1/2 oz)
Baking powder 1/2 tsp

1. Using an electric mixer, beat egg, vanilla essence and chocolate emulco. Cover and leave egg mixture to infuse overnight in the refrigerator. Bring to room temperature before use. If time does not permit, leave to infuse at room temperature for 2–3 hours.
2. When ready to bake, preheat oven to 160°C (325°F).
3. Toast hazelnuts and almonds lightly in the oven for about 5 minutes. Leave to cool before halving nuts. Keep them chunky. Set aside. Keep oven heated.
4. Using an electric mixer, beat butter until smooth. Add brown sugar and salt and continue to beat until well combined. Add egg mixture at room temperature, then cinnamon. Stir in oats or cereal, ground almonds, chopped nuts and chocolate morsels/chunks.
5. Sift flour with baking powder and fold it gradually into batter until the right consistency is achieved. The dough should not be too stiff or too wet. If all the flour has been added and the dough is still wet, add a little more flour.
6. Using a teaspoon, scoop spoonfuls of dough onto ungreased baking trays, spacing them slightly apart.
7. Bake each batch for 10–12 minutes or until edges are nicely browned. Leave to cool completely before storing in airtight containers.

NOTE

- The dough will be easier to handle if it is chilled for about 15 minutes before moulding. For the best results, keep the dough refrigerated while a batch of cookies is baking.
- Adjust the baking time to achieve the cookie texture you crave. A little less time in the oven produces chewier cookies while a little more time makes them crispy.

KEK KUKUS

Makes one 25-cm (10-in) square cake

Other than being a food caterer, my mother also used to teach Quran recital. I remember a lady who paid only a token sum of a dollar a month for her son's lessons five days a week. When he graduated from basic Quran recital to the Quran, my mother bought him a Quran. Being only nine, I asked her why since the Quran cost more than what she was paid. She replied that "real kindness and generosity is doing something nice for people and hoping they will never find out." I will always remember my mother for her kindness and generosity. During Eid, she would make at least five of these steamed fruit cakes to give away even though it takes over 4 hours to produce each of these gems. We recently discovered that she had willingly shared this precious family recipe with a relative who owns a bakery in Malaysia, getting nothing in exchange. It doesn't surprise me at all. That was the kind of person she was.

Plain (all-purpose) flour 465 g (1 lb $^1/_2$ oz)
Bicarbonate of soda 1 tsp
Cream of tartar 1 Tbsp
Mixed dried fruit 350 g (12$^1/_2$ oz)
Blackcurrants 450 g (1 lb)

Pure creamery butter 500 g (1 lb 1$^1/_2$ oz), at room temperature
Vanillin powder $^1/_2$ tsp
Castor sugar 300 g (11 oz) + 230 g (8$^1/_5$ oz)
Eggs 5, medium
Baking powder 1 tsp

1. Lightly grease a 25-cm (10-in) square baking tin, then line with non-stick baking paper, leaving an overhang on two opposite sides to help unmould cake when done. Bring water to boil in a steamer.
2. Sift flour with bicarbonate soda and cream of tartar into a bowl. Add mixed fruit and blackcurrants and mix well. Coating fruit with flour will prevent them from sinking to the bottom of cake. Set aside.
3. Using a large bowl and a wooden spatula, beat butter with vanillin powder and 300 g (11 oz) sugar until light and fluffy.
4. In another bowl, whisk eggs with baking powder, adding one egg at a time until well combined.
5. Add egg mixture to butter mixture gradually, mixing until well combined. Add flour and fruit mixture. Stir well.
6. Melt 230 g (8$^1/_5$ oz) sugar in a non-stick pan over low heat until bubbles start to form. Let sugar bubble over until mixture turns dark brown. Immediately add to batter, stirring quickly with a wooden spatula.
7. Pour batter into prepared tin and cover with aluminium foil. Place in steamer and steam for 4 hours over high heat. Leave to cool before removing cake from tin.

NOTE

- The melted sugar will harden when it touches the batter, so stir quickly. Do not worry if there is some crystallised caramel in the batter.
- Check the level of water in the steamer from time to time and top up as necessary. When topping up water in the steamer, add boiling water so the heat is kept consistent.

COOKIES & CAKES 151

KEK MARMAR

Makes one 23-cm (9-in) square cake

There are many variations to this classic marble cake but this recipe produces a cake that will remain soft and creamy even after it has cooled. In fact, it tastes even better the day after baking. Whenever my mother made this cake for sale, she would involve all the four of us because we enjoyed taking turns to pour the batter into the baking tin. For our own consumption, my mother would set aside just enough batter to fill a small baking tin. Although small, the little cake was something we treasured and the highlight of each baking session.

Cake flour 270 g (9$^{2}/_{3}$ oz)
Baking powder 1/2 tsp
Baking soda 1/4 tsp
Cocoa powder 2 Tbsp
Hot water 2 Tbsp
Chocolate paste 1 tsp
Unsalted butter 300 g (11 oz), at room temperature
Vanillin powder 1 tsp
Castor sugar 280 g (10 oz)
Eggs 5

1. Preheat oven to 170°C (330°F). Lightly grease a 23-cm (9-in) square baking tin, then line with non-stick baking paper, leaving an overhang on two opposite sides to help unmould cake when done.
2. Sift cake flour, baking powder and baking soda together. Set aside.
3. Dissolve cocoa powder in hot water, then stir in chocolate paste. Set aside.
4. Using an electric mixer at medium speed, whisk butter, vanillin powder and sugar until smooth. Lower speed and add eggs one at a time while whisking continuously.
5. Add flour mixture and stir well.
6. Divide batter into 2 portions. Add chocolate mixture to one.
7. Pour a ladleful of plain batter into prepared baking tin, then top with a ladleful of chocolate batter. Repeat to pour batters alternately into prepared baking tin until batters are used up. Shake tin gently to spread batter and get rid of any air bubbles.
8. Bake for 50–60 minutes or until a skewer inserted into the centre of cake comes out clean.
9. Leave cake to cool completely in tin before unmoulding. Slice to serve.

NOTE

- This cake can be stored in the refrigerator for a longer shelf life.

COOKIES & CAKES 153

KEK POTONG BISKUT COKLAT DAN KISMIS

Makes about 16 squares

These chocolate biscuit and raisin squares are quick and easy to make. They are the ultimate no-bake cake. Just pop the tin into the refrigerator for it to set. I started making this treat when I was studying in Manchester, UK. At the hostel where I lived, there was no oven and I was really craving to bake. Today, this is my go-to recipe whenever I am strapped for time and unable to prepare an elaborate cake.

Dark chocolate 150 g (5$^1/_3$ oz)
Milk chocolate 50 g (1$^2/_3$ oz)
Unsalted butter 200 g (7 oz)
Golden syrup 2 Tbsp
Cocoa powder 1 Tbsp
Seedless jumbo raisins 50 g (1$^2/_3$ oz)
Apricots 40 g (1$^1/_3$ oz), cut into small pieces
Dried cranberries 30 g (1 oz)
Toasted almond slivers 60 g (2$^1/_4$ oz)
Digestive biscuits 200 g (7 oz), broken up into 3–4-cm (1–1$^1/_2$-in) pieces

1. Lightly grease a 20-cm (8-in) square baking tin and line with non-stick baking paper.
2. Place dark chocolate, milk chocolate and butter in a double boiler or a bowl placed over a pot of boiling water. Stir until melted. Add golden syrup and cocoa powder and continue stirring until well mixed.
3. Mix together raisins, apricots, cranberries, almonds and biscuits. Pour into chocolate mixture and mix well.
4. Press mixture into prepared baking tin. Refrigerate for 2–3 hours or until firm.
5. Cut into 16 squares. Keep refrigerated until ready to serve.

NOTE

- Vary this simple no-bake cake by using different types of dried fruit and nuts.
- The squares can be decorated by dusting with icing (confectioner's) sugar if desired.

KEK BROWNIE TIGA-COKLAT KACANG WALNUT

Makes one 23-cm (9-in) square cake

Brownies, once familiar only in Western countries, can now be found in many Malay households in Singapore. This triple chocolate walnut brownie has a rich, dense texture, something of a cross between a cookie and a cake. It is not too chocolatey in taste and is very popular with both children and adults. Serve it warm with a scoop of ice cream.

Walnuts 50 g ($1^{2}/_{3}$ oz), chopped and toasted
Dark chocolate 250 g (9 oz)
Unsalted butter 125 g ($4^{1}/_{2}$ oz)
Soft brown sugar 185 g ($6^{2}/_{3}$ oz)
Eggs 3
Grated orange zest 1 tsp
Plain (all-purpose) flour 125 g ($4^{1}/_{2}$ oz)
Cocoa powder 30 g (1 oz)
Milk chocolate chips 100 g ($3^{1}/_{2}$ oz)
Dark chocolate chips 100 g ($3^{1}/_{2}$ oz)
White chocolate chips 100 g ($3^{1}/_{2}$ oz)

1. Lightly grease a 23-cm (9-in) square baking tin, then line with non-stick baking paper, leaving an overhang on two opposite sides to help unmould cake when done.
2. Preheat oven to 150°C (300°F). Place walnuts on a baking tray and toast lightly in the oven for about 5 minutes. Leave to cool before chopping.
3. Increase oven temperature to 170°C (330°F).
4. Place dark chocolate and butter in a double boiler or a bowl placed over a pot of boiling water. Stir until melted. Set aside.
5. Using an electric mixer, beat soft brown sugar with eggs until thick and fluffy. Add grated orange zest, then fold in melted chocolate mixture.
6. Sift plain flour with cocoa powder, then stir into chocolate mixture.
7. Add milk, dark and white chocolate chips and walnuts.
8. Pour mixture into prepared baking tin. Bake for 40–45 minutes or until a skewer inserted into the centre of cake comes out clean.
9. Leave brownie to cool in tin before unmoulding. Slice to serve.

NOTE

- Baking the brownie at a moderate temperature (170°C / 330°F) will yield a lovely, moist cake. The brownie will have a slightly soft centre when it is freshly baked, but this will firm up as it cools.
- If your preference is for chunkier pieces of chocolate in the brownie, replace the chocolate chips with chopped chocolate.

SNACKS & DRINKS

Teh Ceylon Halia Mamu Nazeer 160

Santan Durian 162

Onde-Onde 164

Kuih Bakar Berlauk Hubaba 168

Bubur Kacang Hijau 170

Air Bandung Soda 172

Air Nenas 174

Air Mata Kucing 176

TEH CEYLON HALIA MAMU NAZEER

Makes 5–6 small servings

Many Malay cookies and cakes are usually baked for festive occasions such as Eid, but there is also a wide range of other desserts and drinks that can be served any day. In this section are some of the typical favourites that can be prepared with minimal inconvenience. I have also selected some unique recipes, some of which have special significance to my family. This drink, for example, which I've named after my father, is a metaphorical portrayal of him. It celebrates his Ceylonese heritage and his fixation on ginger as a root with health benefits.

Water 1 litre (32 fl oz / 4 cups)
Ceylon tea leaves 2 tsp
Ginger 5-cm (2-in) knob, peeled and roughly chopped
Sugar to taste

1. In a heavy saucepan, boil water with Ceylon tea leaves for about 10 minutes.
2. Add ginger and allow it to infuse to desired taste.
3. Strain tea through a filter.
4. Add sugar to taste. Serve hot.

NOTE

- If Ceylon tea is unavailable, black tea leaves can be used as substitute.
- If desired, stir 2 Tbsp sweetened condensed milk into the tea, then pour the tea back and forth from one cup to another to form a nice froth before serving.

SANTAN DURIAN

Serves 5–6

This durian in creamy coconut milk is such a delicious example of how fruit is used in Malay desserts. Durian is known in South East Asia as the king of fruit and it is loved for its rich and sweet taste. This saccharine dessert can be eaten on its own but my late uncle Syed Abdullah Sani always loved eating it with some glutinous or plain rice.

Water 400 ml ($13^{1}/_{3}$ fl oz)
Sugar 100 g ($3^{1}/_{2}$ oz)
Coconut milk 200 ml (7 fl oz)
Pandan leaves 2, tied into a knot
Palm sugar (*gula melaka*) 200 g (7 oz)
Durian 5–6 seeds with flesh

1. In a heavy saucepan over low heat, stir water and sugar continuously until sugar is dissolved.
2. Add coconut milk and continue to simmer. Do not bring mixture to the boil.
3. Add pandan leaves. Stir gently.
4. Remove pan from heat and let mixture cool for about 10 minutes before adding block of palm sugar. Stir and let sugar dissolve to desired sweetness, then remove palm sugar.
5. Pour mixture into a large serving bowl. Add durian.
6. Serve warm or cold. To serve cold, add ice cubes.

SNACKS & DRINKS 163

ONDE-ONDE

Makes about 30 balls

Onde-onde is a traditional *kuih* or snack made either from sweet potatoes or glutinous rice flour. My mother's recipe uses glutinous rice flour and the extract of pandan leaves. This snack is a pleasure to eat as the balls pop in your mouth, releasing the sweet sensation of the melted palm sugar.

Pandan Juice
Pandan leaves 5, cut into short lengths
Water 150 ml (5 fl oz)

Dough
Salt 1/2 tsp
Hot water 225 ml (7 1/2 fl oz)
Glutinous rice flour 300 g (11 oz)
Palm sugar (*gula melaka*) 200 g (7 oz), cut into small pieces
Green food colouring (optional)

Coating
Grated skinned coconut 200 g (7 oz)
Salt 1/2 tsp
Pandan leaves 3, cut into short lengths

1. Prepare pandan juice. Place leaves with water in a blender and process until fine. Pass mixture through a sieve or strainer to extract pandan juice. Set aside.
2. Prepare dough. Stir salt into hot water. Combine glutinous rice flour, salted water and pandan juice. If a darker green dough is preferred, add a drop of green food colouring. Mix well into a soft dough. The dough should not stick to your fingers. Add more flour if necessary.
3. Form dough into small balls about 2.5-cm (1-in) in diameter.
4. Using your thumb, make a depression in the centre of a dough ball and spoon in some palm sugar. Bring edges of dough up around filling and enclose. Repeat until dough is used up. Set aside.
5. Place grated coconut in a steaming tray. Sprinkle salt over and toss in cut pandan leaves. Steam for 10 minutes, then set aside to cool. Have steamed grated coconut ready for coating cooked dough balls.
6. Fill a large saucepan with about 2 litres (64 fl oz / 8 cups) water and bring to the boil. Keep water at a rolling boil as you cook the dough balls.
7. Gently drop a few balls into boiling water. The balls are cooked and ready when they change colour and float to the surface. Allow balls to float for a minute before scooping them up with a sieve or perforated ladle. Drain off excess water and place on bed of grated steamed coconut. Coat balls well with grated coconut.
8. Leave balls to sit for 5–10 minutes before serving to allow melted sugar filling to cool.

NOTE

- If fresh grated coconut is unavailable, fine desiccated coconut could be used as an alternative.
- When forming the balls after filling with palm sugar, be sure to seal them well to prevent the palm sugar from seeping out when melted.

SNACKS & DRINKS

KUIH BAKAR BERLAUK HUBABA

Makes about 70 pieces

This recipe is from my mother-in-law who used to conduct cooking classes attended by up to 50 students each time. Although she does not teach anymore, my mother-in-law is still very willing to produce these gems and share her recipe with anyone who asks for it. This spiced beef snack is quite simple to do, but you will need a special *kuih bakar* mould which is easily available from traditional Asian baking shops.

Plain (all-purpose) flour 300 g (11 oz)
Eggs 4, beaten
Salt to taste
Coconut milk 850 ml ($28\frac{1}{3}$ fl oz)
Yellow food colouring $\frac{1}{4}$ tsp
Pandan leaf 1, tied into a knot to be used as a brush
Ghee or vegetable oil for greasing mould

Topping
Vegetable oil as needed
Minced beef 500 g (1 lb $1\frac{1}{2}$ oz)
Onions 2, peeled and cut into small cubes
Garlic 3, peeled and cut into small cubes
Ginger 1-cm ($\frac{1}{2}$-in) knob, peeled and thinly sliced
Meat curry powder 1 Tbsp
Salt to taste
Coriander leaves (cilantro) 15 g ($\frac{1}{2}$ oz), finely chopped
Spring onions (scallions) 15 g ($\frac{1}{2}$ oz), finely chopped
Red chillies 3, sliced

1. Prepare topping. Heat some oil in a wok and add minced beef, onions, garlic, ginger and curry powder. Season with salt to taste. Stir-fry until mixture dries up. Drain excess oil and set aside.
2. In a large bowl, combine flour, eggs, salt, coconut milk and food colouring. Mix well. Run batter through a sieve to remove any lumps.
3. Using the pandan leaf brush, grease *kuih bakar* mould with some ghee or oil.
4. Place mould on stove and heat. Fill each cup with batter and leave to cook for about 5 minutes before topping each cake with some minced meet, coriander, spring onions and a slice of red chilli.
5. Continue to cook for another 20 minutes until batter is cooked through. Remove cakes from mould and repeat to make more cakes until ingredients are used up.
6. Serve warm.

BUBUR KACANG HIJAU

Serves 4–6

Mung beans or *kacang hijau* are commonly used in South East Asian cooking especially in Chinese cuisine, as well as in Japanese, Korean and Indian cuisines. It is common to see Chinese desserts being adapted into Malay cuisine and one common adaptation is *bubur kacang hijau*, a sweet dessert with the consistency of porridge. The beans are cooked with sugar, coconut milk and palm sugar and flavoured with pandan leaves. As with most great cooks, my mother knew how to modify and use leftovers to create other dishes. Whenever there was any excess of this sweet mung bean dessert, she would make it into another traditional snack, *kuih gendang kasturi* (sweet mung bean fritters).

Mung beans 250 g (9 oz)
Water 1.5 litres (48 fl oz / 6 cups)
Pandan leaves 3, tied into a knot
Coconut milk 200 ml (7 fl oz)
Palm sugar (*gula melaka*) 100 g (3^1/$_2$ oz), grated
Castor sugar 100 g (3^1/$_2$ oz)
Salt to taste

1. Rinse mung beans thoroughly under running water to remove any impurities.
2. Place water, mung beans and pandan leaves in a heavy saucepan. Bring to the boil, then lower heat and simmer, stirring, for about 30 minutes or until beans are soft. Top up with more water if necessary while cooking.
3. Add coconut milk, palm sugar and castor sugar and simmer for another 10 minutes. Beans should be soft but not mushy. Season with salt to taste.
4. Continue to cook until mixture thickens. Remove from heat.
5. Ladle into individual serving bowls and serve hot.

NOTE

- A 2.5-cm (1-in) knob of ginger can be added while simmering the beans for additional flavour.

SNACKS & DRINKS 171

AIR BANDUNG SODA

Makes 6–8 glasses

Air bandung soda is a popular beverage among Malay communities. It is made by mixing rose syrup or cordial with evaporated milk and served with ice. There are many different variations to this drink and my mother's recipe uses sweetened carbonated water, adding a pleasant fizzy twist to this common drink. Other modern innovations include adding grass jelly and tapioca pearls.

Rose syrup 125 ml (4 fl oz / 1/2 cup)
Water 700 ml (23 1/3 fl oz)
Evaporated milk 150 ml (5 fl oz)
Sweetened carbonated water 180 ml (6 fl oz / 3/4 cup)
Ice cubes as desired

1. Mix rose syrup with water, then stir in evaporated milk, mixing well.
2. Add sweetened carbonated water and stir to combine.
3. Pour into glasses over ice cubes and serve.

NOTE

- The sweetened carbonated water gives this drink its unique taste, but should it not be available, omit using it or replace with a carbonated drink.

AIR NENAS

Makes 6–8 glasses

Pineapple is a versatile fruit in Malay cooking. It is used in sweet and savoury dishes as well as in drinks such as this pineapple drink or *air nenas*. My mother used to pour this drink into plastic tubes, then freeze and sell them for 20 cents per tube. There would be children queuing at our front door to buy this frozen treat. I sometimes also make this drink and freeze some into popsicles as a treat for my children. They are a refreshing change to the ice creams that we get commercially.

Water 1 litre (32 fl oz / 4 cups)
Sugar 100 g ($3^1/_2$ oz)
Pandan leaves 5, tied into a knot
Pineapple 400 g ($14^1/_3$ oz), cut into small pieces
Yellow food colouring $^1/_2$ tsp
Vanilla essence $^1/_2$ tsp
Ice cubes (optional)

1. Place water, sugar and pandan leaves in a heavy saucepan. Bring to the boil, stirring to dissolve sugar.
2. Add pineapple slices and food colouring.
3. Remove from heat. Leave to cool for a few minutes before adding vanilla essence. Stir and mix well.
4. Serve warm or chilled with ice cubes.

SNACKS & DRINKS 175

AIR MATA KUCING

Makes 6–8 glasses

The recipe for this dried longan drink is very simple but it plays a significant role in my family. It is the drink that we serve to all our guests on the first day of Eid every year without fail. As my father is the oldest in the family, we receive hundreds of visitors just on the first day of Eid. My mother believed that we should not serve fizzy drinks to our guests after they had fasted for a month, thus she always prepared this drink for them. It is a perfect thirst quencher and is refreshing at the same time.

Dried longan 50 g ($1^{2}/_{3}$ oz), rinsed
Water 500 ml (16 fl oz / 2 cups)
Sugar 100 g ($3^{1}/_{2}$ oz)
Pandan leaves 2, tied into a knot
Ice cubes (optional)

1. Place dried longan and water in a heavy saucepan and bring to the boil. Boil until longan is softened.
2. Add sugar and pandan leaves. Stir well to dissolve sugar.
3. Remove from heat and set aside to cool.
4. Serve warm or chilled with ice cubes.

GLOSSARY OF INGREDIENTS

ANCHOVIES, DRIED Better known as *ikan bilis* in Malay, these whitebait range from 2–5 cm (1–2-in) in length and are sold dried and preserved in salt. Dried anchovies are highly versatile as an ingredient—they can be used to make stock, to season dishes and are also often deep-fried to make a side dish.

BANANA LEAVES In Asian cooking, banana leaves are typically used as food wraps for the subtle hint of flavour and aroma they infuse after steaming or grilling. To make the leaves pliable and easy to fold, place the leaves over an open flame or a pot of boiling water until softened. Banana leaves can generally be found in Asian grocery stores and supermarkets. If unavailable, aluminium foil or parchment paper can be used as an alternative.

CANDLENUTS Also known as *buah keras* in Malay and *kemiri* in Bahasa Indonesia. Unlike other nuts, candlenuts are never eaten raw or on their own, but are typically ground with other ingredients and cooked, acting as a thickener in stews and gravies. Macadamia nuts, raw almonds or cashews can be used as substitutes for candlenuts as they have similar high oil content and texture.

CARDAMOMS Cardamoms have a spectrum of complex flavours, ranging from slightly sweet with citric elements to spicy. These fruit pods each contain approximately 10 to 15 intensely aromatic black seeds. Whole pods can be bruised lightly using a mortar and pestle prior to use. Ten pods can produce approximately 1^{1}/$_{2}$ tsp ground cardamom. If a recipe calls for ground cardamom, it is best to grind the seeds just before using as their flavour and aroma are quickly lost if the spice is pre-ground.

CHILLIES There are typically three types of chillies used in South East Asian cooking—fresh finger-length chillies, bird's eye chillies and dried chillies. Fresh green and red chillies (above) are the size and length of fingers and are usually moderately hot. Deseeding will lessen their level of spiciness. Adjust the number of chillies used according to taste. Bird's eye chillies (right) are also known as *cili padi*. They are about 4-cm (1^{1}/$_{2}$-in) in length and are fiery hot.

CHILLIES, DRIED Dried chillies are used to add a piquant flavour to dishes. Soak them in hot water for about 10 minutes to soften before use. Remove the chilli stalks, then cut into short lengths before blending or pounding. Twenty dried chillies and 150 ml (5 fl oz) water can produce approximately 10 Tbsp dried chilli paste.

CLOVES Cloves emit a strong distinctive flavour and are used in the preparation of many dishes around the world. They are one of the spices added to spice blends such as Chinese five-spice powder and Indian curry powder. Due to their strong flavour, it is best to follow the recommended quantities stipulated in recipes to avoid altering the taste of the dish.

COCONUT, SKINNED AND GRATED Fresh grated coconut flesh is indispensable in many authentic Malay dishes. This is one ingredient that should not be substituted. However, should the fresh ones be unavailable, desiccated coconut can be used as a substitute.

COCONUT MILK This creamy white milk is an essential ingredient in Malay cooking. It is what gives Malay dishes and desserts their rich flavour and fragrance. Coconut milk is best extracted from fresh grated coconut, but if grated coconut is unavailable for this, some supermarkets stock refrigerated packets of fresh coconut milk and coconut milk in cartons which make good alternatives.

CORIANDER LEAVES (CILANTRO) Also known as Chinese parsley, coriander leaves are favoured for their strong fragrance and can be used as an ingredient in cooking or raw as a garnish. This fresh, green herb is highly perishable and should be used within a day or two of purchase. If storing is necessary, keep it wrapped in newspaper in the refrigerator.

CUMIN SEEDS Belonging to the parsley family, cumin seeds have a distinctive aroma which makes them a popular spice used in various spice blends and curry pastes. Its flavour can be accentuated by toasting. As cumin seeds are similar in shape to fennel seeds, they are sometimes mistaken for fennel seeds, although cumin seeds are smaller and darker in colour.

CURRY LEAVES Curry leaves add a distinct flavour and aroma to an assortment of dishes, especially Indian curries. They are typically sold fresh in sprigs at Asian grocery stores. Fresh curry leaves are the best choice but if unavailable, dried curry leaves can be used. The dried leaves are milder and more leaves may be needed to achieve the desired flavour.

FENNEL SEEDS These small, slightly curved seeds vary in colour from brown to light green. They are also called sweet cumin or large cumin because they resemble cumin seeds. Fennel seeds have a licorice-like flavour and like cumin, fennel seeds are popularly used in spice blends and curry pastes in Malay cooking.

GALANGAL Also known as *lengkuas*, galangal belongs to the same family as ginger but it has a citrus flavour and possesses a more intense aroma then ginger. It is used either fresh or ground. Grinding 100 g (3½ oz) fresh galangal with 100 ml (3½ fl oz) water yields approximately 10 Tbsp galangal paste.

GHEE Ghee is a class of clarified butter originating from the Indian subcontinent. It is made by removing milk solids from butter and thus keeps well at room temperature for extended periods. When unavailable, butter can be used as a substitute.

KAFFIR LIME LEAVES Also known as *daun limau purut* in Malay, these dark green leaves emit an intense citrus aroma and can be used whole or finely shredded. When shredding, remove the stiff central vein. If the fresh leaves are not available, the frozen or dried leaves can be used as a substitute.

LEMON GRASS Popularly known as *serai*, lemon grass emits a refreshing flavour and aroma that makes it an essential ingredient in many spice blends. To use, peel away the tough outermost layer, then trim the two ends. The desired part of the lemon grass is the bulbous end. If the recipe calls for the stalk of lemon grass to be used whole, bruising or crushing it helps release its flavour. Grinding 4 stalks of lemon grass with 150 ml (5 fl oz) water yields approximately 10 Tbsp paste.

PANDAN LEAVES When used in savoury dishes and desserts, pandan leaves impart a subtle green hue, and a unique sweetness and aroma. Similar to banana leaves, they are often used to wrap ingredients or are typically tied into a knot before adding to the pot. Bottled pandan essence or vanilla essence can be used as substitutes in dessert recipes, but for savoury dishes, it is best to exclude them when unavailable.

PALM SUGAR Also known as *gula melaka*, this variety of palm sugar is available in dark brown cylindrical blocks. Palm sugar has a faint caramel flavour that can be best substituted with brown sugar or maple syrup if it is unavailable. Prior to use, palm sugar can be grated or chopped to reduce cooking time.

PRAWNS (SHRIMPS), DRIED A popular ingredient in Asian cooking, these small sun-dried saltwater prawns are typically available in Asian markets. Although dried, they are best stored refrigerated to retain their freshness. Rinse, then soak the required amount in water for 10–15 minutes to soften and remove excess salt before use.

GLOSSARY OF INGREDIENTS

PRAWN (SHRIMP) PASTE, DRIED (BELACAN) Dried prawn paste is made from fermented prawns that are sun-dried, then pounded into a concentrated paste. The result is a highly pungent paste shaped into rectangular blocks or round slabs. To enhance its flavour prior to use, wrap the required amount in aluminium foil, then roast in the oven or dry-fry in a wok until dry and fragrant.

PRAWN (SHRIMP) PASTE, BLACK Made of fermented prawns, salt and sugar, this thick black paste is known locally as *petis* or *haeko*. It is a basic ingredient in many Malay sauces and dips.

TAMARIND PULP This sweet-sour pulp found in tamarind seed pods is used extensively in Malay cuisine. Some recipes require tamarind juice to be made from the pulp. This is achieved by mixing the pulp with water, then straining out the fibre and seeds before use.

TURMERIC This underground rhizome is easily identified by its bright yellow-orange flesh. It is typically used in marinades and spice mixtures, and is valued for its ability to mask fishy smells. Commercially available in fresh or ground form, 1 Tbsp ground turmeric can be substituted with 100 g (3 1/2 oz) turmeric root.

TEMPEH Tempeh originates from Indonesia and is made from compressed and fermented soy beans. Although it is also made from the basic ingredient of soy beans, tempeh differs in flavour and texture from bean curd. Its high nutritional content of protein, dietary fibre and vitamins appeals to the health conscious, and hence it is typically available in health food stores today.

MENU SUGGESTIONS

Special Family Meals

Mee Rebus (page 72)
Bol Kentang Hajjah Zabidah (page 100)

Nasi Lemak Meal
Nasi Lemak (page 50)
Sambal Tumis Udang (page 94)
Ayam Goreng Berempah (page 36)
Kangkong Belacan (page 126)
Bergedil (page 108)

Nasi Goreng Kampung Cili Hijau Meal
Nasi Goreng Kampung Cili Hijau (page 60)
Sate Ayam (page 34)
Mahshi Kobis Hubaba (page 130)

Nasi Putih (Many dishes included in this book can be served as side dishes to plain rice (nasi putih). Suggestions are indicated in the recipes. The suggestion below is a special combination which takes time to prepare, but is worth all the effort.)
Rawon (page 106)
Sambal Goreng (page 112)
Sambal Jengganan Che Zahara Kaum Ibu (page 122)
Bergedil (page 108)
Serunding Daging (page 110)
Sambal Belacan (page 31)

Festive Occasions

Lontong Sayur Lodeh Meal
Lontong Sayur Lodeh (page 58)
Rendang Daging (page 104)
Sambal Tumis Udang (page 94)
Sambal Goreng (page 112)
Kari Ayam Melayu (page 116)
Serunding Daging (page 110)
Sambal Kacang (page 30)

Nasi Jagung Meal
Nasi Jagung (page 64)
Paceri Nenas (page 134)
Kurma Ayam (page 114) or
   Ayam Masak Merah (page 118)
Sambal Tumis Udang (page 94)

Small Home Parties

Finger Foods
Epok-Epok Daging (page 38)
Roti Mariam (page 40)
Samosa Daging Berempah (page 44)
Sate Ayam (page 34) with Sambal Kacang
   (page 30)

Main Courses
Nasi Ayam (page 54) with Chap Chye
   (page 128)
Nasi Pulau (page 62) with Sambal Tumis Udang
   (page 94)
Roti Kirai (page 70) with Kari Ayam Melayu
   (page 116)
Soto Ayam (page 68) with Bergedil (page 108)

Desserts and Snacks
Kek Brownies Tiga-Coklat Kacang Walnut
   (page 156)
Kek Kukus (page 150)
Kek Marmar (page 152)
Kek Potong Biskut Coklat Dan Kismis (page 154)
Santan Durian (page 162)
Onde-Onde (page 164)
Kuih Bakar Berlauk Hubaba (page 168)
Bubur Kacang Hijau (page 170)

WEIGHTS & MEASURES

Quantities for this book are given in Metric, Imperial and American (spoon) measures. Standard spoon and cup measurements used are: 1 tsp = 5 ml, 1 Tbsp = 15 ml, 1 cup = 250 ml. All measures are level unless otherwise stated.

Liquid and Volume Measures

Metric	Imperial	American
5 ml	1/6 fl oz	1 teaspoon
10 ml	1/3 fl oz	1 dessertspoon
15 ml	1/2 fl oz	1 tablespoon
60 ml	2 fl oz	1/4 cup (4 tablespoons)
85 ml	2 1/2 fl oz	1/3 cup
90 ml	3 fl oz	3/8 cup (6 tablespoons)
125 ml	4 fl oz	1/2 cup
180 ml	6 fl oz	3/4 cup
250 ml	8 fl oz	1 cup
300 ml	10 fl oz (1/2 pint)	1 1/4 cups
375 ml	12 fl oz	1 1/2 cups
435 ml	14 fl oz	1 3/4 cups
500 ml	16 fl oz	2 cups
625 ml	20 fl oz (1 pint)	2 1/2 cups
750 ml	24 fl oz (1 1/5 pints)	3 cups
1 litre	32 fl oz (1 3/5 pints)	4 cups
1.25 litres	40 fl oz (2 pints)	5 cups
1.5 litres	48 fl oz (2 2/5 pints)	6 cups
2.5 litres	80 fl oz (4 pints)	10 cups

Dry Measures

Metric	Imperial
30 grams	1 ounce
45 grams	1 1/2 ounces
55 grams	2 ounces
70 grams	2 1/2 ounces
85 grams	3 ounces
100 grams	3 1/2 ounces
110 grams	4 ounces
125 grams	4 1/2 ounces
140 grams	5 ounces
280 grams	10 ounces
450 grams	16 ounces (1 pound)
500 grams	1 pound, 1 1/2 ounces
700 grams	1 1/2 pounds
800 grams	1 3/4 pounds
1 kilogram	2 pounds, 3 ounces
1.5 kilograms	3 pounds, 4 1/2 ounces
2 kilograms	4 pounds, 6 ounces

Oven Temperature

	°C	°F	Gas Regulo
Very slow	120	250	1
Slow	150	300	2
Moderately slow	160	325	3
Moderate	180	350	4
Moderately hot	190/200	370/400	5/6
Hot	210/220	410/440	6/7
Very hot	230	450	8
Super hot	250/290	475/550	9/10

Length

Metric	Imperial
0.5 cm	1/4 inch
1 cm	1/2 inch
1.5 cm	3/4 inch
2.5 cm	1 inch

RESOURCES

Books

Abdullah, Kamsiah et al., *Malay Heritage of Singapore*, 2010, Suntree Media in association with Malay Heritage Foundation

Che Zahara Bte Noor Mohamed, *An Appeal from Che Zahara Bte Noor Mohamed, President, Malay Women's Welfare Association*, K.B. Press

Hutton, Wendy, *Authentic Recipes from Malaysia*, 2005, Peiplus Editions

Khoo, Kay Kim, Abdullah, Elinah & Hao, Wan Men, *Malays/Muslims in Singapore: Selected Readings in History, 1819–1965*, 2006, Pelanduk Publications

Lee, Edwin, *The British as Rulers: Governing Multiracial Singapore, 1867–1914*, 1991, Singapore University Press, National University of Singapore

Wong, David & Wibisono, Djoko, *The Food of Singapore*, 2005, Periplus Editions

Websites

National Heritage Board
www.nhb.gov.sg

Malay Heritage Centre
http://www.malayheritage.org.sg

Museums

Asian Civilisations Museum
1 Empress Place
Singapore 179555
www.acm.org.sg

Malay Heritage Centre
85 Sultan Gate
Singapore 198501
www.malayheritage.org.sg

National Museum of Singapore
93 Stamford Road
Singapore 178897
www.nationalmuseum.sg

INDEX

Acar Timun 132
Air Bandung Soda 172
Air Mata Kucing 176
Air Nenas 174
Asam Pedas Ikan 82
Ayam Goreng Berempah 36
Ayam Masak Merah 118

bean sprouts 42, 68, 72, 76, 122
beef 38, 44, 46, 62, 72–73, 78, 96, 100, 102, 104, 106, 108, 112, 114, 116, 124, 128, 130, 168
Bergedil 108
Biskut Coklat Chip Kayu Manis 148
Biskut Coklat Putih Pistachio 146
Biskut Kacang Madu Cornflakes 138
Biskut Suji 142
Bol Kentang Hajjah Zabidah 100
buah keluak (Indonesian black nut) 106
Bubur Kacang Hijau 170

Chap Chye 128
chillies
    bird's eye 31, 42, 54, 60, 68, 76, 90
    dried 30, 36, 50–51, 54–55, 58, 62, 72, 76, 78, 82, 84, 86, 88, 94, 96, 100, 102, 104, 110, 112, 116, 122, 132
    green 40, 58, 60, 72, 112, 114, 116, 126, 132, 134
    red 31, 44, 54, 58, 60, 70, 76, 86, 92, 96, 104, 106, 114, 124, 126, 134, 168
chocolate
    dark 154, 156
    milk 154, 156
    white 146, 156
cocoa powder 152, 154, 156

coconut
    grated coconut 110, 164
    milk 50, 58, 66, 76, 90, 92, 104, 112, 114, 116, 118, 162, 168, 170
cornflakes 138
curry leaves 116, 118
curry/spice powders
    beef curry powder 38, 72, 116
    korma spice powder 114
    meat curry powder 168
    rendang beef powder 104
    soup spices powder 44, 46, 68, 100, 130

durian 159, 162

Epok-Epok Daging 38
evaporated milk 64, 70, 172

galangal 30, 34, 58, 68, 76, 88, 90, 104, 106, 110, 112, 118, 124
ghee 38, 40, 70, 140, 142, 144, 168
glutinous rice 66, 164

Ikan Bungkus Daun Pisang 88
Ikan Goreng Masam Manis 86
Ikan Sumbat Berlada 84

kaffir lime leaves 58, 68, 90, 92, 104, 106, 110
kalamansi limes 88
kangkong 121, 126
Kangkong Belacan 126
Kari Ayam Melayu 116
Kek Brownies Tiga-Coklat Kacang Walnut 156
Kek Kukus 150
Kek Marmar 152

Kek Potong Biskut Coklat dan Kismis 154
Ketam Masak Lemak Cili Padi 90
Kuih Bakar Berlauk Hubaba 168
Kuih Makmur 144
Kuih Tart Klasik 140
Kurma Ayam 114

ladies fingers 82
Laksa Johor Nani 76
laksa leaves 76, 82, 84
lemon grass 30, 34, 58, 68, 76, 82, 84, 88, 90, 104, 106, 110, 112, 118
long beans 58, 122
Lontong Sayur Lodeh 58

Mahshi Kobis Hubaba 130
Mee Rebus 72
Mee Telur Daging 78

Nasi Ayam 54
Nasi Goreng Kampung Cili Hijau 60
Nasi Jagung 64
Nasi Lemak & Sambal Tumis Ikan Bilis 50
Nasi Pulau 62

Onde-Onde 164

Paceri Nenas 134
palm sugar (*gula melaka*) 30, 62, 110, 112, 162, 164, 170
pandan leaves 30, 50, 54, 64, 66, 70, 140, 162, 164, 168, 170, 174, 176
pineapple 86, 134, 140, 174
Plain Rice 30
potatoes 38, 100, 108, 114, 116
Pulut Kuning 66

Rawon 106

Rendang Daging 104
rose syrup 172
Roti Kirai 70
Roti Mariam 40

Sambal Belacan 31
Sambal Goreng 112
Sambal Jengganan Che Zahara Kaum Ibu 122
Sambal Kacang 30
Sambal Sotong Daging Sumbat 96
Sambal Tumis Udang 94
Samosa Daging Berempah 44
Santan Durian 162
Sate Ayam 34
sauces/pastes
    black prawn (shrimp) paste 42
    dried prawn (shrimp) paste 31, 42, 50, 58, 72, 76, 82, 92, 94, 96, 112, 122, 126
    fermented prawns (shrimps) (*cincalok*) 88
    sweet soy sauce 42, 68, 72, 78, 124
    tomato ketchup 44, 70, 78, 86
Semur Daging 124
Serunding Daging 110
Soto Ayam 68
sweetened condensed milk 140

Tahu Goreng 42
tamarind pulp 30, 34, 42, 50, 62, 82, 84, 94, 96, 110, 122
Teh Ceylon Halia Mamu Nazeer 160
tempeh 58, 112, 122
Traditional Lontong 31
turmeric 58, 82, 84, 90, 104, 106, 110
turmeric leaf 58, 84, 90, 104, 110

Udang Bakar 92

PHOTO CREDITS

All photographs by Hongde Photography except as indicated below:

Bernard Go: Top three images on page 6 and page 21 (scenes of the Malay Village at Geylang Serai) and page 137 (right)

Ministry of Information, Communications and the Arts/National Archives of Singapore: Third inset image on the front cover (the Satay Club at the Esplanade, 1985)

National Archives of Singapore: Second inset image (a satay seller, 1952) and fourth inset image (a Malay food stall at a funfair held at the Bukit Panjang Government School, 1952) on the front cover, page 22 and back cover (cooking for a Hari Raya Haji celebration at Kampong Sarhad, 1986)

Rita Zahara: Pages 10, 11, 12, 13, 14, 15, 16, 17, 23, 24, 25 and 27

Singapore Tourism Board/National Archives of Singapore: First inset image on the front cover (customers at a Malay food stall selling snacks)

ABOUT THE AUTHOR

Rita Zahara

Rita Zahara is a bilingual TV presenter, newsreader, TV producer, TV director, lecturer, scriptwriter, journalist, entrepreneur and bestselling cookbook author. Rita's journalistic experience and her prominence among the Malay community makes her the perfect candidate to represent the community as well as to compile this legacy of recipes passed down from her late mother and grandmother. Rita grew up around food as her late mother was a caterer and to her, cooking is the way of life she was born into. With a lifelong passion for food and cooking, Rita continues to expand her presence in the culinary world. She has produced several television cooking programmes, and in 2012, she launched her own line of cookies and cakes—*Che Zahara by Rita Zahara*. Rita also conducts cooking workshops and hosts culinary heritage discovery trips. She has been invited to conduct numerous cooking demonstrations island-wide and has been a judge/panelist for several food festivals in Singapore and the region.

Rita was the creative consultant for the Singapore Food Festival 2012 and was also in charge of the masterclasses for some 10 celebrity chefs. Most recently, Rita was invited to attend the Malaysian Food Festival in Sydney, Australia, where the recipes in this book were featured. Rita was also a guest author at the Singapore's Writers Festival 2012.

Rita's versatility is evident in how she juggles her many responsibilities on top of running two integrated transmedia agencies—AteR LLP and ReTA Pte Ltd. Rita remains passionate about human culture and contributes to Mendaki's Community Leaders Forum aimed at enhancing Malay/Muslim standing in society. She is also on the board for many government-aided agencies and is heavily involved in humanitarian work for Muslim communities in South East Asia, empowering women and children with access to education. Rita often conducts inspirational talks for adults, youths and children. Rita engages her audience on her blog and Facebook page https://www.facebook.com/RitaZaharaPAGE.

CONTRIBUTORS

From left: Rita Zamzamah, Rita Zuhaida, Rita Zarina and Rita Zahara

Rita Zarina is currently pursuing a Master's degree in Education at the Nanyang Technological University, National Institute of Education (Singapore). She is trained in Special Needs Education and has been a teacher in a local secondary school for the past 12 years. As a former teacher counsellor, she remains attentive to the needs of her students and volunteers as a mentor to youths and youths-at-risk. Rita Zarina also has a keen interest in Malay script writing for television programmes.

Rita Zamzamah currently lives with her husband and 3-year-old daughter in Tokyo where she is pursuing a PhD in International Studies under the Japanese government's Monbukagakusho scholarship. Since her teenage years, Rita Zamzamah has been heavily committed to improving the lives of the less fortunate through community service. For this, she was conferred the Raffles Junior College KD Gupta Award for Excellence in Community Service, the Singapore Children's Society Commendation Award and the Ministry of Community Development and Sports (MCDS) Long Service Award in Community Service. She also received a British Petroleum scholarship for excellence in community service and education.

Rita Zuhaida is the youngest of the four sisters. She has just completed her Bachelor's degree in Accountancy but her interest is not limited to accounting. Her passion lies in working with youths and she is taking small steps to make a difference in the Malay/Muslim community. To this end, she has collaborated with various organisations to spear-head activities for youths. Having lost her mother to kidney failure, she has since also developed a deep compassion for the less fortunate and devotes her time to caring for the welfare of kidney patients.